Henry Darling

The Closer Walk

The Believer's Sanctification

Henry Darling

The Closer Walk
The Believer's Sanctification

ISBN/EAN: 9783337417512

Printed in Europe, USA, Canada, Australia, Japan

Cover: Foto ©Lupo / pixelio.de

More available books at **www.hansebooks.com**

THE

CLOSER WALK

OR

THE BELIEVER'S SANCTIFICATION.

BY

HENRY DARLING, D.D.

PHILADELPHIA:
J. B. LIPPINCOTT & CO.
1862.

Entered according to Act of Congress, in the year 1862, by
J. B. LIPPINCOTT & CO.
In the Clerk's Office of the District Court of the United States for the Eastern District of Pennsylvania.

PREFACE.

This little volume does not aspire to a place in the libraries of the learned. Its ambition is not for fame, but usefulness.

It is addressed to those who have commenced *walking* with God; and its simple purpose is to incline them to a *closer* and *habitual* communion with Him, and to show them how such a fellowship may be attained.

That in our religious literature there is a want of a volume with this special aim,—a volume characterized by a simplicity of thought and style that will make it intelligible to *all*, and at the same time free from those theological *novelties* which have marred some modern treatises upon this subject,—the author of these pages has long felt. That they will *fully* supply this want he dares not hope. It is, however, towards this end that they aim.

For *any* minister of Christ to desire the extension of his usefulness beyond the limits of a single congregation, and for this reason to employ the facilities of the press, is neither unnatural nor presumptuous. But how much is the desire in this way to do something for his Master strengthened when, by the afflictive providence of God, a minister is *temporarily* exiled from all other fields of usefulness! No longer permitted, as he was wont, with his *voice* to speak for Christ, he can hardly refrain from speaking through the printed page in His name.

It is perhaps due to himself, that the author of this volume should say that its preparation and publication are entirely owing to such a fact in his personal history.

May God add His blessing!

H. D.

PHILADELPHIA, April 22, 1862.

CONTENTS.

CHAPTER I.
Sanctification—Its Meaning.................................... 7

CHAPTER II.
Sanctification—Its Character..................... 22

CHAPTER III.
Progress—An Essential Characteristic of True Piety 36

CHAPTER IV.
Progress in Holiness—How it is Evinced..... 50

CHAPTER V.
Sanctification—How Attained......................... 68

CHAPTER VI.
Sanctification—Through Suffering............... 85

CHAPTER VII.
Paul—An Example of Sanctification............ 104

CHAPTER VIII.
Paul's Sanctification—The Method of its Attainment 121

CHAPTER IX.
The Great Motive to Sanctification 142

CHAPTER X.
Connection between Holiness and Usefulness 154

CHAPTER XI.
Progress in Religion Essential to Prevent Declension 175

CHAPTER XII.
Assurance of Hope—Its Relations to Sanctification 184

CHAPTER XIII.
Holiness Here—Its Connection with Glory Hereafter 196

CHAPTER XIV.
Holiness the Great Necessity of the Church 210

The Closer Walk.

CHAPTER I.

SANCTIFICATION—ITS MEANING.

> "Saviour! though my rebellious will
> Has been by thy blest power renewed,
> Yet in its secret workings still
> How much remains to be subdued!"
> CHARLOTTE ELLIOTT.

"Furthermore then we beseech you, brethren, and exhort you by the Lord Jesus, that as ye have received of us how ye ought to walk and to please God, so ye would abound more and more."—1 THESS. 4: 1.

WHEN our blessed Saviour was about to leave His sorrowing disciples, He offered in their behalf, to His heavenly Father, the prayer, "Sanctify them through thy truth." That they had already entered upon the divine life, and were at heart the sincere followers of Christ, cannot be doubted. The testimony of Jesus is explicit: "Now ye are clean through the word which I have spoken unto you." "They are not of the world, even as I am not of the world."

Paul's earnest desire for the Thessalonian believers—so frequently addressed by the endeared title of "brethren"—was expressed in the words, "The very God of peace sanctify you *wholly;*" and the same apostle rebukes the Jewish converts, who had been for some time Christ's disciples, for "having need"—by reason of the feebleness of their spiritual life—"of milk, and not of strong meat." When Peter was about closing his public ministry,—at least, so far as his inspired writings formed a part of it,—he did so by exhorting all who "had obtained like precious faith with him through the righteousness of God," to "grow in grace;" and the beloved John expresses his conviction of the continually increasing power of true religion in the soul, by the words, "And every man that hath this hope in him purifieth himself, even as He is pure."

The work of grace upon the heart is not, then, completed when the soul first yields itself to the dominion of Jesus, and from His enemy becomes His friend. There is something more in religion for a man to desire and seek after than an entrance, however truthful, upon God's service. Conversion—or a turning from sin to holiness—is not a final, but an initial work. It is only the first step in a path that is afterwards to be patiently travelled, or the first victory over an enemy that must in the future on many a battle-field be met and conquered. We greatly dishonor Christ's earthly mission if we ever conceive of it as having any lower purpose than "that He might redeem us from *all* iniquity, and purify unto Himself a peculiar people, zealous of good works."

To designate what is thus accomplished

in the soul by the grace of God, subsequent to its truthful entrance upon the divine life, the word *sanctification* has generally been employed. It includes, therefore, in its meaning, all the steps in religion but the first, and all the victories of the soul over sin, save that one which is fought at the very outset of its spiritual career.

But the work comprised under this term needs, in order to be properly understood, a fuller explanation; and this we can give in no better way than by inquiring into the condition of an individual at the moment when he has been enabled, by divine grace, to exercise a true faith in Christ. The first step in a Christian life taken, what are our relations to God, and what is our inward spiritual state?

Complete justification is a result that immediately follows the hearty acceptance of Christ as our Saviour. "There is therefore now no condemnation to them which are in

Christ Jesus." The answer of Peter to the question of the convicted Jews at Pentecost, "Men and brethren, what shall we do?" was, "Repent, and be baptized every one of you in the name of Jesus Christ for the remission of sins." The very moment a sinner accepts of the finished work of Christ in his behalf, his sins, which were many, are forgiven; he is, for Christ's sake, accounted as righteous; and that law which before could be satisfied only by his eternal death, has now no claims against him.

And this justification is in its very nature complete. It admits of no increase or decrease. It can never be greater or less. *Perfect* at its beginning, it can never make any advancement. The aged disciple who is in character, as well as years, "quite on the verge of heaven," is no more fully pardoned, or more free from the condemning sentence of the law, than the young convert whose spiritual birth was but yesterday.

How difficult is it for us to realize this truth! and the practical forgetfulness of it, into what a bondage to fear does it bring many a believer!

But, such the relations of the soul to God the moment it exercises true faith, what is its inward spiritual state? "Whosoever believeth that Jesus is the Christ, is born of God." "Therefore, if any man be in Christ, he is a new creature: old things are passed away; behold, all things are become new." That same faith which, by reason of the relations of Christ's atonement to God's law, is the condition of our complete justification, becomes, for the same reason, a power for our inward regeneration.

Few truths are more frequently or beautifully taught us in the sacred Scriptures than this *double* work of Christ in our behalf. In the old Levitical economy—which was "a shadow of good things to come"—there were two kinds of offerings which were always to go together. The first, or burnt-offering, was a bloody sacrifice, and a holocaust; the second, or meat-offering, a bloodless oblation, and only partly consumed by fire. One was propitiatory, the other eucharistic. In the one, we behold penitence laying its hand on the head of the innocent sufferer, and praying to be spared for that sufferer's sake; in the other, gratitude making its return for the unspeakable gift, by the dedication to God of the offerer's person or property. The burnt-offering was a kind of fact-picture of that divine sacrifice by which alone sin could be pardoned; the meat-offering, a beautiful symbol of the forgiven sinner's willing and cheerful presentation of himself to God's service.

In that incident in Christ's crucifixion related by John,—"But one of the soldiers with a spear pierced His side, and forthwith came there out blood and water,"—it is quite possible that some Bible-readers see only a singular pathological phenomenon; but the inspired apostle marks it as memorable and significant. In his Gospel he repeats it with a triple asseveration; and when, in old age, he sat down to write his Epistles, he indicates its spiritual importance by again referring to it, in the language, "This is He that came by water and blood, even Jesus Christ; not by water only, but by water and blood." The incident, then, was a symbol of some great truth; and, as *blood* in the Old Testament Scriptures is always used to denote expiation, and water to symbolize purity, we are constrained, in that baptismal flow from the pierced side of Jesus, to recognize the two great and indissoluble benefits of justification and regeneration which we derive from His death.

And how strikingly is the same fact shadowed forth in the two sacraments of the Church! Indeed, what are these but twin emblems of these twin benefits? That sacra-

SANCTIFICATION—ITS MEANING. 15

mental water which in baptism falls upon the brow, like those holy drops which followed from the spear of the Roman soldier, has as its verity that change which is wrought in the heart by the grace of Jesus Christ. It is emblematic of purity. It signifies the sanctifying influences of the Holy Ghost. While the bread and wine which in the Supper is broken and poured out, like that blood which crimsoned the beloved side of Jesus on the cross, has as its verity the great truth that "He was wounded for our transgressions, and bruised for our iniquities."

But here, in closely examining that inward spiritual state into which the believer is by faith brought, we observe that in one particular it differs very essentially from that relation to God which the same faith has established. The justification that follows immediately upon the sinner's acceptance of Christ is, as we have already remarked, *complete*. But this is not so with that inward and spiritual change which is simultaneous with justification.

The term most generally employed in the sacred Scriptures to denote this change is a *new birth;* and that in its very nature implies the possibility—if not the necessity—of progression. Life is perhaps never, save in the reality of its existence, a complete thing at first. It has its beginning, usually small and feeble, and its subsequent stages of fuller and stronger development. In the vegetable world there is "first the blade, then the ear, and after that the full corn in the ear;" and in the animal world life has its various stages of infancy, youth, manhood, and old age.

And the same idea is implied in the term " new creature," which inspiration has sometimes employed in speaking of this change. At the first exercise of His creative power, God made few things in the material world with all that completeness that we now behold in them. Time elapsed ere they were fully fashioned and formed. This beautiful world itself was once " without form and void, and darkness was upon the face of the deep ;" and even after " the Spirit moved upon it," it was only in periods widely separated from each other that it successively became the home of its present almost endless variety of plants and animals.

And with this agree the whole history of the Church, and the personal experience of every believer. If that spiritual change which is the result of the first act of faith was perfect and complete, then would its subject never afterwards lapse into sin; then Job would never, even for a moment, have complained of God's ways, David would never have been guilty of the heinous crime of adultery, and Peter have never denied his Master.

Upon this supposition, there would also have been no room for those earnest longings after God and holiness that so pre-eminently characterized Bible saints. Then the Psalmist would not have exclaimed, "My soul thirsteth for God, for the living God: when shall I come and appear before God?" nor would he have uttered those words, so expressive of present unrest, "I shall be satisfied, when I awake, with thy likeness."

Nor yet, again, could the believer's life be a battle,—a constant struggle with sin,—if his regeneration was so complete as to leave within him no remnants of depravity. Delighting "in the law of God after the inward man," Paul, upon the supposition that we are considering, could not have still "seen another law in his members, warring against the law of his mind, and bringing him into captivity to the law of sin which was in his members."

Why, also, those exhortations addressed to believers, "Watch and pray, that ye

SANCTIFICATION—ITS MEANING.

enter not into temptation;" "Take unto you the whole armor of God, that ye may be able to withstand in the evil day;" or those petitions contained in the prayer taught by Christ to His disciples, "Lead us not into temptation, but deliver us from evil;" if regeneration is not an initial work, and if, after its blessed experience by the soul, there are not temptations to be met, spiritual conflicts to be waged, and a higher degree of inward purity to be attained?

Here, then, is the precise meaning of *sanctification*. Having to do with a soul which has already been pardoned and regenerated, in which the life of Christ has been commenced, it is that life going onward and upward to perfection. It is in the spiritual world what manhood is to infancy, or what the full corn in the ear is to the blade, in the natural. It is "perfecting holiness in the fear of the Lord." It is having "every thought and feeling brought into captivity to the obedience of Christ." It is "being filled with all the fulness of God," becoming perfect even as our Father which is in heaven is perfect, and, "leaving the nursery and its pattering by rote of elementary truths, it is proceeding to the attainment of a vigorous maturity in truth and holiness."

It should, perhaps, be here remarked that the meaning just given to the word "sanctification" is rather theological than Biblical. The sacred writers, in their use of it, do not, ordinarily, exclude the first step in the divine life, but employ it as comprehending all that is done by the agency of God's Spirit in reclaiming men from their apostasy, and in preparing them for heaven. As when the tabernacle and the altar, with the vessels that pertained to them, withdrawn from all profane uses and solemnly set apart to the worship of Jehovah alone, were said to be sanctified, so, when a sinner is separated from the world and attached to the service of God, the whole work of his salvation is frequently designated in the sacred Scriptures by the same term.

But this general and comprehensive use of the word, is in no way opposed to the limited signification we have given it. Indeed, the same thing is true of all the terms employed by inspiration to denote the work of God upon the soul. With a specific meaning, a peculiar appropriateness to designate some particular part of the great work, they are still generically employed. The very moment, however, we attempt to isolate any portion of that work and distinctively to speak of it, we rightfully come back to these terms and employ them in their specific meaning. And this is just what we have done with regard to the word "sanctification."

CHAPTER II.

SANCTIFICATION—ITS CHARACTER.

> "The faith that unites to the Lamb,
> And brings such salvation as this,
> Is more than mere notion or name:
> The work of God's Spirit it is,—
> A principle, active and young,
> That lives under pressure and load,
> That makes out of weakness more strong,
> And draws the soul upward to God."

"First the blade, then the ear, after that the full corn in the ear."—MARK 4: 28.

WE have already indicated, in our attempts to define sanctification, one of its peculiar features. It is progressive. Into a gracious state we come instantaneously. Every man must be either the friend or the enemy of God, and must sustain such a relation to the divine government as to be, at any moment, either received into paradise, or doomed to endless misery in hell. The first step in the divine life is never slow and tedious. The soul may have been long in preparing for it, but the actual turning from sin to holiness is a single and an immediate act. One moment "dead in trespasses and sins," the next we are "new creatures in Christ Jesus."

But once in a gracious state, our future spiritual advancement is progressive. IN GRACE WE GROW. The principle of holiness, implanted in the soul at regeneration, is afterwards perfected in the fear of the Lord; and, the foundation of Christian character then laid, we are subsequently "built up a spiritual house."

We have already said of life that it is never perfect at its commencement: we may now add the remark that it never becomes so instantly, or at a single development. Infancy never reaches manhood by a single leap, nor does the blade at once ripen into the full ear. We plant our seed-corn in the ground, and say, "It is yet four months, and then cometh harvest." Life develops itself, it is true, with very different degrees of rapidity, sometimes so quickly as to startle us, and again so slowly as to occasion some measure of impatience. Nature has its aloes and its ephemera, its plants of a century and of a day's growth; yet in each is there progression. And is it otherwise with divine life? Are there in this analogy, so pre-eminently Scriptural, no points of resemblance?

In one of the Psalms, the sacred poet, speaking of the believer's life, compares it to one of those stately palm-trees that Oriental travellers behold standing in the plains or on the mountain-sides of Judea, "like military sentinels, with their feathery plumes nodding gracefully on their proud heads." "The righteous shall flourish like the palm-tree." What a truthful, as well as beautiful, picture does this inspired similitude give of the gradual progress of a believer in holiness! "The palm grows slowly, but steadily, from century to century, uninfluenced by those alternations of the seasons which affect other trees. It does not rejoice overmuch in winter's copious rain, nor does it droop under the drought and the burning sun of summer. Neither heavy weights which men place upon its head, nor the importunate urgency of the wind, can sway it aside from perfect uprightness. There it stands, looking calmly down upon the world below, and patiently yielding its large clusters of golden fruit, from generation to generation."*

But, while sanctification is progressive in its character, this progress is not always, nor perhaps generally, uniform. The waxing of the morning light,—a divine similitude to illustrate the path of the just— Christian character is, still, not ordinarily

---

* The Land and the Book, vol. i. p. 65.

developed with such perfect regularity. Believers sometimes seem suddenly to make very great advances in holiness. Out of some terrible affliction, or from some marked deliverance from danger, they come greatly invigorated in all the graces of the divine life. Indeed, as Christians, they now hardly seem to us to be the same individuals as before. They have lost their spiritual identity, in their suddenly awakened and greatly invigorated Christian graces.

And, doubtless, facts like these constitute one ground for the opinion, entertained by some, that sanctification is not progressive, but is a kind of "second conversion," or a "higher Christian life," reached in a moment by the soul. Yet precisely the same phenomenon is frequently seen in the developments of the mind. Under the pressure of peculiar circumstances, the intellect, ordinarily maturing slowly and with much uniformity, has been known, almost in a moment, to leap from a position of comparative obscurity and weakness, into one of the highest influence and power.

That commissioner of the Scottish Kirk to the Westminster Assembly,—George Gillespie,—who rolled back the tide of Erastianism in that body with an eloquence and learning that seemed almost fabulous, came forth, like a brilliant meteor, out of comparative darkness. It was the fearful danger in which the *truth of God* was then placed, that stimulated his intellect, unloosed his tongue, and made him, though much the youngest member of the Assembly, "one of its most able and ready debaters, encountering not only on equal terms, but often with triumphant success, the most learned, subtle, and profound of his antagonists."

Let none of our readers, then, forget this peculiar feature of sanctification. Instead of being the work of a day, it is the believer's spiritual vocation for life. It is something that, as Christians, we are to do continually. All the circling hours of our being are to be the periods of its exercise. It is a work to be begun, continued, and, in this life, never ended. Its full and glorious consummation will not be reached till, separated from all outward contact with evil, and the world's weight lifted from the soul, it shall have entered the mansion prepared for it from the foundation of the world. "The souls of believers are at their death made *perfect in holiness*, and do immediately pass into glory." (Shorter Catechism, Q. 37.)

And this slowness of achievement, and tardiness of the final result, it must be confessed, is the most trying and disheartening fact in our spiritual life. Men enlist for a life-battle far more reluctantly than for a summer's campaign; and run with less alacrity in a race when the goal is distant than when it is just at hand:

> "If but this tedious battle could be fought,
>   With Sparta's heroes, at one rocky pass,—
> One day be spent in dying,—men had sought
>   The spot, and been cut down like mower's grass.
> If in the heart of nature we might strive,
>   Challenge to single combat the great power,
> Welcome the conflict! But no! half alive,
>   We skirmish with our foe long hour by hour."

But, while this is true, let it not be forgotten that in this battle every onward movement is a *glorious victory*, not only because it helps on the final consummation, but because in itself it glorifies God, and promotes our own highest happiness.

But, in addition to this peculiar feature of sanctification, there is another, worthy of special notice. *It is a growth.* We are all familiar with two ways in which objects increase in this world. Some progress by a vital force within. They have an inherent power of self-enlargement. Others increase only by external and outside additions. A tree is an illustration of the first of these methods of increase; a house, of the second. In the one there is a vital, self-active principle, which, carefully selecting new matter and taking it into its own organization, by some subtle process of digestion and assimilation, leads it continually to deepen its roots, enlarge its trunk, and send out wider and wider its branches. In the other there is no internal power of production, but every increase of volume is wrought entirely by the application of external force. The first is a growth; the last, a mere mechanical enlargement.

Now, of these two methods of increase, sanctification, as a progressive work, belongs wholly to the first. The tree, and not the house, is its truthful type. Men are never built up in holiness as the architect adds stone to stone in his edifice, each new block having no necessary affinity with those upon which it is laid. True Christian progress is always a *growth*. It is the natural efflorescence of a spiritual life divinely imparted to the soul. That rich cluster of heavenly graces that we sometimes behold adorning the character of a matured believer—just like that golden fruit which in summer we see hanging from the tree's branches—is the natural and necessary outgrowth of his new and spiritual life.

And how beautifully is this characteristic of sanctification illustrated in the various similitudes that are employed to describe it in the sacred Scriptures! These—with rare exceptions—are living, active things, and such as possess inherently the capacity of growth. The believer is "like a tree planted by the rivers of water, that bringeth forth his fruit in his season." "The kingdom of heaven is like to a grain of mustard-seed, which a man took and sowed in his field." "I am the vine, ye are the branches." "Henceforth be no more children, . . . but speaking the truth in love, *grow* up into

Him in all things, which is the head, even Christ." Indeed, so full are the sacred writers of this idea, that when employing an image that would not naturally admit of it,—that is itself dead and inanimate,—they yet sometimes constrain it—if we may so speak—to embody this conception. Thus, when Paul speaks of Christ as the corner-stone of the Church, and all believers as necessarily built upon Him and constituting a part of His spiritual house, the figure is in itself clearly one of simple superposition. Yet observe how, by an almost improper use of words, he vitalizes it: "In whom all the building, fitly framed together, GROWETH unto an holy temple in the Lord."

To this view of the character of sanctification we should add—not, it is true, as an essential and necessary characteristic of it, but as one highly desirable—that it should be symmetrical. All the graces of the Christian life should be harmoniously and proportionally developed. None should be dwarfed, none overgrown. *Zeal* should not outstrip *knowledge,* nor behind knowledge should *virtue*—a manly courage equal to all duty—ever lag. With love to God *brotherly-kindness* and *charity* should go hand in hand; and he who has been strong to do for his Master should not be less *patient* to endure for Him.

In that beautiful passage in Peter's Second Epistle where the apostle exhorts all believers to "add to their faith, virtue, knowledge, temperance, patience, godliness, brotherly-kindness, charity," the reference, as scholars tell us, in the word rendered in our version "*add*," is to a choir of well-trained musicians; and *as* each of these faithfully fulfils his part,—as no one is remiss in his duty, but all together blend their notes in faultless harmony,—*so* all the graces of the Christian life, supplementing each other, and together forming one complete whole, should be "*added*" one to another. It is not to the cultivation of a single isolated grace that the apostle here calls believers, but to the symmetrical development of all.

And, to enforce this exhortation, we may perhaps safely say that no more beautiful or convincing exhibition of Christian character can be made to the world than this. Every mind delights in symmetry. Its presence in the human form is essential to beauty. It constitutes the highest charm of the fine arts. We can have no true music without chords, no good poetry without rhythm, and no painting without harmony of colors. "The *completeness* of the moral system propounded by Christ is a mark of its divinity;" and so is that character which in all its parts has been fashioned by it.

But, alas! such spectacles are rare. Sanctification—a progressive work, a growth—is still seldom symmetrical. We cannot oftentimes truthfully describe a Christian's character by simply linking together the various graces of the believer's life. Candor frequently requires that we should separate them. We say: "He is a good man, kind and charitable, *but* rough and irritable in manner. He is temperate and patient; *but* he lacks charity. He is reverent and devout; *but* he is entirely destitute of steadfastness and moral courage."

Old countries—such as Greece and Rome—are full of buildings which are partly regal and partly rustic, their front adorned with Corinthian columns and a carved entablature that belonged to the age of Pericles or Augustus, but their roof and sides of the rudest modern art. Not unlike these edifices is oftentimes Christian character. Solid and valuable qualities are united with weak and valueless ones; graces that charm us by their beauty, lie close by the side of defects that repel us.

CHAPTER III.

PROGRESS—AN ESSENTIAL CHARACTERISTIC OF TRUE PIETY.

> "Rivers to the ocean run,
> Nor stay in all their course;
> Fire, ascending, seeks the sun:
> Both speed them to their source.
> So a soul that's born of God
> Pants to view His glorious face,
> Upward tends to His abode
> To rest in His embrace."

"But the path of the just is as the shining light, that shineth more and more unto the perfect day."—PROV. 4: 18.

THE *possibility* of progress in holiness, on the part of those who have just entered upon the Christian's race, will, perhaps, be universally admitted; nor are there many who would deny this possibility to any believer at any subsequent stage in his heavenly journey. Few men regard either themselves or others as possessed of a complete Christian character. They admit that before them are heights of piety still unreached, and within them imperfections that still need to be eradicated.

And, as in the moral government of God the true measure of responsibility is ability, this possibility of progress, it is readily conceded, constitutes its duty. Men are solemnly bound to do and to be for Christ every thing that they can. He only is a faithful servant to whom the Master can say, as to the woman who in the house of Simon poured the ointment of spikenard upon His head, "She hath done what she could."

But, still further, all will admit that every believer is in the Bible solemnly commanded to make progress in holiness. "Grow in grace" is the Scriptural injunction to all its recipients. No man has a right forever to remain "a babe in Christ," but is continually exhorted by the voice of inspiration to look forward to and to strive after that glorious period when he shall come unto a perfect man, unto the measure of the stature of the fulness of Christ. The condition of the gift of holiness is its cultivation. Piety, divinely implanted in the soul at regeneration, is "a talent;" and he who will not "put it to the exchangers"—who will not double it by diligent watching and prayer, so that his Lord may at "His coming receive His own with usury"—must meet the doom of the unprofitable servant.

Two things, then, with reference to Christian progress may be regarded as admitted; *its possibility, and its duty.* Believers MAY advance in holiness: they have the capacity of spiritual progress. Believers OUGHT to advance in holiness: God solemnly commands it.

But can we stop here? Is this an exhaustive statement of our theme? Is Christian progress a possibility, and a duty, ONLY? Do we speak the whole truth when we say that a child of God MAY and OUGHT to grow in grace? We are bold to affirm the incompleteness of the statement. There is a *necessity* in Christian progress, as well as a possibility and a duty, and a *must* in the believer's advancement in holiness, as well as a *may* and an *ought*.

Progress is an essential characteristic of true piety. It belongs to its very essence. It is one of its inherent qualities. It is as inseparable from it as the capacity to burn is inseparable from fire, or as the tendency to throw out light is inseparable from a luminous object.

This is measurably true of all religions, even the false, when sincerely believed. Towards the character of the object worshipped, that of the worshipper *must* constantly progress. Looking at his God as the standard of perfection, and, consequently, condemning and seeking to eradicate from his own character whatever is unlike that, every man is necessarily changed into His image: he becomes like his God. And as this process must go on in the soul just as long as the Deity remains the object of the man's supreme homage, *so* must he ever grow into conformity to Him.

Moreover, as every worshipper desires the favor of the object worshipped, and as reason dictates that this can be obtained only by conformity to the will and character of that object, it is obvious that *self-interest*, as well as the fact just mentioned, is continually promoting in man an assimilation of character to his God.

How full of sad evidence to this truth is the whole history of the idolatrous world! The ancient Egyptians were brute-worshippers, and bestiality—the lowest vice to which human nature can descend—was common among them. In bowing down to "birds, and four-footed beasts, and creeping things," they sunk themselves to the lowest depths of vice. Odin and Thor—the divinities of the Scandinavians—were hero-kings, bloodthirsty and cruel; and hence in the bosoms of that fierce race of Northmen the milk of human kindness seemed to be turned into gall. Venus—the personification of lust—was the goddess of Corinth; and, as a necessary consequence, her inhabitants were proverbial for dissoluteness.

How exact these parallels! Whole nations in moral character precisely like the divinities they worship! It is said that the Chinese have this truth as a kind of proverb: "Think of Buddha, and you will be transformed into Buddha. If men pray to Buddha and do not become Buddha, it is because the mouth prays, and not the mind."*

And what is thus true of all false religions, is it not equally true of Christianity? Poor, benighted pagans becoming assimilated in

---

* Philosophy of the Plan of Salvation, p. 23.

their moral character to the various objects which they worship,—becoming like Odin and Thor and Venus and Buddha,—can it be otherwise with the Christian? Must not he become like the august object of his worship,—*like Jehovah?* "And every man that hath this hope in him purifieth himself, even as He is pure."

But, again, that progress is an essential and inherent characteristic of true piety, is evident from the fact—already frequently referred to—that Christianity is a life. When you take a *living* seed and cast it into the ground, you do not say that it *may* grow, or that it *ought* to grow, but that it *must* grow. It is its very nature not to remain as it is, but to unfold continually new forms of life and beauty; and nothing but the entire destruction of the living principle within it can prevent this result. Even though some superincumbent mass may for a while retard and hinder it in its growth, yet will it struggle for the light, and, sending out in every direction its roots, finally lift itself above the earth.

Precisely thus is it with religion. If the beginning of piety in the soul were like a stone cast into a well, it might indeed be otherwise. We might then speak of the believer's progress in holiness as a possibility *only*. As, however, that beginning finds its true type in the living seed, we cannot speak of the Christian's progress as any thing but an inherent necessity. And hence, in that beautiful parable of our Lord in which the commencement of true religion, either in the world or in the heart of the individual believer, is said to be "like to a grain of mustard-seed, which a man took and sowed in his field," Christ immediately adds, "which indeed is the least of all seeds: but when it is grown, it is the greatest among herbs, and becometh a tree, so that the birds of the air come and lodge in the branches thereof."

But we have not yet concluded our argument on this point. Between the various stages of progress that may be said to intervene from the commencement of the believer in the divine life, to his final and complete sanctification, there is a most *interesting* and *vital connection*. None are isolated. None stand alone, but *all* are so intimately allied that they perpetually call each other into being. Their mutual relations are not unlike the various links of a chain, so that, taking hold of one, the others, by a kind of natural sequence, follow. Just as we sometimes say in regard to an unregenerate man who has taken the first step in sin, that this leads on, by a sort of moral necessity, to a long series of transgressions, is it with every advance made by the believer in the way of holiness. It draws him on towards, and almost certainly secures, other advances.

To illustrate this thought. A child of God increases in *knowledge*. He has obtained a fuller perception of the divine character than he has ever enjoyed; and, as a necessary consequence, his emotion of holy *love* is at once greatly inflamed. The better vision of his God perfects within him the grace of Christian *love*. But then, in return, this awakened and increased love brings God nearer to his soul; and thus does the process continually repeat itself. Knowledge and love perpetually call each other into new and brighter existence.

And thus is it with all the graces of the new life. No one will walk alone and unattended in the soul. They are a sisterly choir, and delight too much in the fellowship of each other to be separated. If a man increase in his confidence towards God,—if his *faith* in Him be strengthened,—his affection for Him will be correspondingly enlarged. If he love Him more, his *hope* will be confirmed. If he have a firmer conviction that there remains for him a crown hereafter, he will be more *patient* to bear present trial. If he truly love God, he will love his brother also.

Should any planet in our solar system suddenly lose its centrifugal force and be wholly given up to the influence of the centripetal, it would commence a direct movement towards the sun; but this movement, every advance however small, would accelerate, both by the increased momentum that the body has thus acquired, and by the increased attraction to which it would be subjected. Not unlike this is the movement towards God of a soul in which that power of sin which would lead it to fly away from Him, has been effectually destroyed. It carries over from every stage in its progress an acquired momentum that prepares it for the next; while at the same time, advancing by every progression nearer and nearer to God, the attraction of His love is continually augmented.

In thus speaking of progress as an essential characteristic of true piety, we do not, of course, mean to say that it is spontaneous, something that comes of itself, and hence does not need attention and culture. This is seldom true of any life, and never of the divine. "Giving all diligence, add to your faith," is the Scriptural injunction. Because the delicate exotic needs, in order to its growth, the most careful cultivation,—must be shielded from the rough wind and cold, and supplied with abundant sunshine and moisture,—men do not conclude that it is any less a living plant, nor suppose that growth is not one of its inherent qualities. Yet precisely this would we do in religion, if from the acknowledged fact that Christian progress requires on the part of every believer, in order to secure it, the most diligent labor, we should infer that growth was not of all true piety an essential feature.

We repeat, then, our proposition: Christian progress is not a possibility only, but a necessity. True believers not only *may*, and *ought* to, grow in grace, but they *must*. Religion in the soul is a living, vital, active principle. "The righteous also *shall* hold on his way; and he that hath clean hands shall be stronger and stronger."

But, taking this principle with us into the Church of Christ, and making a practical application of it to the real life of God's professed people, how melancholy is the result! With some,—perhaps we might say with many,—ten, twenty, thirty years have been spent in Christ's service and yet no progress has been made. All that time has passed since the soul felt the first celestial breathings of the life of God,—since it started, an infant in the faith,—and yet that poor and feeble childhood remains. They are yet minors in holiness, have not yet come to age, nor assumed the full rights and privileges of a heavenly citizen. What were faults of character, blemishes, sins, at the commencement of their Christian life, are faults still. Then impatient, irritable, censorious, avaricious, the same imperfections now tarnish their character. Is it possible, then, that their conversion was genuine? Has the life of God ever been commenced in their souls? We tremble when we think of the reply that divine truth constrains to be made to these inquiries.

CHAPTER IV.

PROGRESS IN HOLINESS—HOW IT IS EVINCED.

"Religion in its *rise* interests us almost exclusively about ourselves; in its *progress*, it engages us about the welfare of our fellow-creatures; in its more advanced stages, it animates us to consult on all things, and to exalt to the utmost of our power, the power of God."—Rev. C. Simeon.

"For behold this selfsame thing, that ye sorrowed after a godly sort, what carefulness it wrought in you, yea, what *clearing of yourselves.*"—2 Cor. 7: 11.

ALL life has its infallible marks of development, its indices, which, whenever they clearly appear, prove incontrovertibly that it is passing on from infancy to maturity. In the animal world, this is, generally, an enlargement of physical proportion; in the vegetable, the same fact is conjoined with others more specific and peculiar. The blade of corn manifests its growth by the ear that is gradually formed upon it; the wheat, by its bearded head; the plant, by the unfolding of its buds; and the tree, by the mellowing of its fruit.

We are rarely in doubt as to whether life, in any of these various forms, is really in the process of development. In no case, indeed, is its unfolding so manifest as to be palpable to our senses at the very moment of its occurrence. We do not see the tree grow; nor does the flower-bud burst into full bloom the instant that we gaze upon it. The lapse of time seems to be essential to the perception of growth.

Precisely thus is it with the life of God in the soul. It has *its indices*,—suited, of course, to its internal and spiritual character,—yet equally definite and marked with those which distinguish other growths, and, like them, clearly perceptible at intervals more or less distant. What these are, it is our present purpose to endeavor to show, Progress in holiness, how is it evinced?

Our blessed Lord indicates one way, in that oft-repeated declaration, "Whosoever exalteth himself shall be abased; and he that humbleth himself shall be exalted." Great piety is like great knowledge, always connected with humility. Men go down in their own esteem, as in character they approach the divine. He who has the clearest apprehension of God has the most truthful and vivid sense of his own imperfections. "I have heard of thee," said Job, "by the hearing of the ear; but now mine eye seeth thee: wherefore I abhor myself, and repent in dust and ashes."

The Apostle Paul, when he was first converted, said, "I am not worthy to be called an apostle;" when he had made greater progress in holiness, he said, "I am the least of all saints;" but just before he died, when his views of heaven were brightest and his knowledge of himself the clearest, he exclaimed, "I am the chief of sinners."* Eliphaz, Job's friend, uttered many an unwise, and even untruthful, sentiment, in his discourses to the patriarch; but this saying is not among them: " When men are cast down, then thou shalt say, *There is lifting up.*"

As believers progress in holiness, their *religious emotions*, also, become more *disinterested*. In the religious life of a young convert every thing is personal and subjective. His thoughts are mainly upon himself, and he is conscious of little else save his own sinfulness and the redemption which is in Christ Jesus. Even those rapturous feelings of gratitude and adoration sometimes felt by the youthful believer, and which the older disciple of Christ longs after when he exclaims,

> "Oh for the blessedness I knew
> When first I saw the Lord!"

---

* Voices of the Night, p. 180.

are, to a great extent, occasioned by a view of the grace of God as manifested in *his salvation.*

But this absorption of thought upon self cannot long continue if the soul advance in the divine life. Personal interests provided for, and personal anxieties abated, the believer comes more and more out of himself. The chief characteristic of his piety becomes its *objectiveness.* He delights in the contemplation of Christ's character, in the study of His word, and in the examination of divine truth.

A profound axiom of Christian experience is contained in the remark of a Scotch divine, " that one of the most unequivocal signs of ripeness of Christian character is a growing fondness for the *doctrines* of the gospel, as distinguished from its precepts." In that period of mental repose which follows the first and more anxious years of the Christian life, the believer extends the range of his meditations, and soars over the whole realm of moral truth. He looks backward as well as forward; and even those themes which in their logical order precede revelation have to him a special charm.

It is often observed that a mature Christian discipline invests the Old Testament with a peculiar interest, and finds its adoring contemplations naturally expressed in the imagery and language of the Song of Solomon, a book almost without meaning to many a young disciple. Of McCheyne, the Scotch divine, so remarkable for the richness and maturity of his Christian experience, it is said that he had preached so often on the Canticles that at last he had scarcely left himself a single text of its "good matter" which had not been discoursed upon.*

And with this is conjoined a desire, most intense and consuming, for the salvation of

---

* McCheyne's Life, p. 375.

others. When Paul said to his countrymen, "I could wish that myself were accursed from Christ for my brethren, my kinsmen according to the flesh," he was no novice in the school of Christ. Such disinterestedness of religious emotion was the result of long culture. He could not, we are quite sure, have uttered such language when, in all the fervor of his "first love," he entered the city of Damascus.

The great philanthropist Wilberforce, at a time when every energy of his being was absorbed in the effort to secure the abolition of the slave-trade, was asked by a friend if he had not been neglecting his personal prospects and endangering his soul. His magnanimous answer was: "I do not think about my soul. I have no time for thoughts of self. I have really forgotten all about my soul." It was when the disciples of Christ were but half baptized with His spirit, and before that prayer of their Master in their behalf was offered, "Sanctify them through thy truth," that they proposed to Him the selfish inquiry, "Lo, we have left all, and followed thee: what shall we have therefore?"

In a shipwreck, when a man tossed upon the angry bosom of the waters first feels that he has found an object, clinging to which he *may* be saved, all is anxiety. He thinks of nothing but of that object's stability, strength, and capacity to save him. He even forgets that others are all around him sinking in the waves. So soon, however, as this question of personal safety is answered,—so soon as he finds himself secure,—his heart is instantly filled with earnest desires for the salvation of others. Indeed, the man *now* forgets himself, and is wholly absorbed in concern and effort for others. Thus is it with the true believer. At the commencement of his religious life, we cannot deem it strange that it is of himself that he thinks; but should it be so always? His feet firmly planted upon the Rock of Ages, should not his deepest concern now be for the vast multitude who are all around him sinking beneath the waves of sin? Such *must* it be whenever there is any real growth in grace. Progress in holiness has as one of its indices an increasing disinterestedness of religious emotion.

And to this we may add, as still another infallible test of Christian advancement, *increased deadness to the world*. As a power for evil, the love of the world has not lost all its influence even upon the truly regenerate soul. It is to professed Christians that the command is addressed, "Be not conformed to this world, but be ye transformed by the renewing of your mind." The young disciple of Christ is not, indeed, in doubt which to choose as *his portion*, the world or his Saviour; nor does he suppose that this earth can make him happy without the blessing and smile of God; but, then, there are in this world so many fair and bright and beautiful things to fill his fancy, and to awaken hopes of enjoyment, that he is very prone to be too highly pleased with the goodly show. The world has still too fast hold upon him. It intrudes upon his closet, pollutes his Sabbaths, and sometimes persuades him to drink of its tasteless streams, when he ought to have quenched his thirst with the sweet waters that flow from Christ, the living Fountain. It never, indeed, converts him into an apostate and treacherous Judas; but it does sometimes make him a fickle and foolish Demas.

But as the Christian advances in the divine life, this love of the world dies, and hence the liability of being drawn away by it into sin lessens. The old nature more and more thrown off, and the new nature more and more put on, the believer becomes more and more disengaged from the passions and affections of earth. As faith sheds on his path the light of heaven, he sees more clearly the emptiness and vanity of those glittering bubbles, with which the world allures and decoys. Its losses affect him less painfully, and he receives its prosperity with a more sober and subdued spirit.

But what is true of this generic form of sin is equally true of all the specific acts which it includes. As the soul goes onward and upward in the divine life, it marks every step of its progress by its increased power to meet and overcome all temptations to sin.

The young Christian is frequently conquered by his spiritual foes. His relapses into sin are numerous. Ignorant to a great extent of the wiles of the adversary, he is often unable successfully to resist them. Clad in the whole armor of God, he yet wields so unskilfully his weapons as, in many an evil day, to be overcome. Moreover, the whole power of the *great law of habit* is, with a young Christian, against his successful resistance of temptation. He is *accustomed* to do evil; and hence it is very hard for him to do good.

It is an interesting fact, in illustration of this remark, that Bunyan, in his "Pilgrim's Progress,"—a book which, as Dr. Arnold says, "seems to be a complete reflection of Scripture, with none of the rubbish of the schools mixed with it,"—has made Christian yield to one of the first temptations that beset him, after at the cross he lost the burden of his sins. How plaintive is the language of his penitence! "Oh, wretched man that I am, that I should sleep in the daytime! that I should sleep in the midst of difficulty! that I should so indulge the flesh, as to use that rest for ease to my flesh, which the Lord of the hill hath erected only for the relief of the spirits of pilgrims!"

And this liability to sin on the part of

young Christians is especially in the direction, either of their natural defects, or of their previously formed sinful habits. Every individual has vulnerable points in his character. There are sins which—in Scriptural language—*easily* beset him, and it is to their practice that Satan particularly allures. Prone, before our conversion, to anger, envy, pride, covetousness, our greatest danger afterwards is in their indulgence. It was the natural self-confidence of Peter, his ardent and impulsive disposition, never properly disciplined into restraint before he became a disciple of Christ, that in that base denial of his Master reappeared to dishonor his apostleship.

Advancing, however, in holiness, these relapses into sin become more and more infrequent. The mature disciple meets temptation with far more steadiness and success than the young convert. "Using the weapons of his warfare, the believer acquires the art of using them better," and, watching the wiles of the adversary, he learns how more skilfully to escape from them. Natural defects of moral character are eliminated as the soul progresses in the divine life, and the power of sinful habits is broken. Petulance softens into amiableness, envy into brotherly-kindness, pride into humility, and covetousness into a large and generous beneficence.

And this mark of Christian progress, how simple! We can hardly mistake it if we would. It calls us to a plain reckoning of our sins. It bids us tell their number. It exhorts us to compare our present with our past sinful relapses. It inquires whether our obedience is becoming more perfect, and whether the imperfections of our character are being gradually eradicated. Provocations to malevolence, pride, anger, impurity, do we *now* as frequently yield to them as we once did? It is impossible, if we are really growing in grace.

But there is one other evidence of Christian progress that we must not fail to notice. When the pious Rutherford, in writing to a friend, subscribed himself "a man borne down and hungry and waiting for the marriage-supper of the Lamb," we all instinctively feel that, if these words were truthful and honest, his soul must, in the maturity of its graces, have been nearly ripe for heaven.

To the fear of dying, the unregenerate man is all his lifetime in bondage; and, though one of the objects of Christ's incarnation is to deliver His people from this thraldom, yet full and complete liberty in this particular is, perhaps, never the immediate result of true conversion. It is *"perfect love"* that "casteth out fear." It is not until the believer feels some assurance of the personal love of Christ, and until the great objects of his faith begin to assume in his vision the aspect of substantial realities, that he views the close of his life with calm, and even joyful, expectations. The attractions of heaven increase as the Christian in the holiness of his character approaches it, and as the strong ties that once bound him to earth are severed.

We should think it almost strange to hear a young Christian, as expressing his own desires, singing that familiar hymn,

> "Jerusalem! Jerusalem!
> Would God I were in thee!
> Oh that my sorrows had an end,
> Thy joys that I might see!"

A better prayer for such a believer would be those words of David: "Oh, spare me, that I may recover strength, before I go hence and be no more." Yet that old hymn beautifully and truthfully expresses the feelings of a mature disciple.

That men sometimes welcome death for reasons very different from this, cannot, indeed, be denied. There are in society disappointed and restless worldlings, men so "whipped of their own guilty conscience" as to feel that life is a burden and earnestly to desire that they might lay it down. Such are all suicides; and to this class belong a much larger number, who, with the same inward unrest, are deterred from the outward crime only by " the dread of something after death."

But between such a desire to depart from earth, and that which characterizes the mature disciple of Christ, how striking the contrast! There is with the latter nothing of a chafed, vexed, or murmuring spirit, but all is sweet, quiet, and meek. The longing for death of a ripened saint is not so much to escape the sufferings and disappointments of life, as to be free from its temptations and sins. He wishes not so much to get away from himself as continually annoyed by a troublesome companion dwelling in his own bosom, as to get near to a friend whom, having not seen, he yet loves with an affection all-absorbing and supreme.

CHAPTER V.

SANCTIFICATION—HOW ATTAINED.

> "ABIDE IN ME! there have been moments pure
> When I have seen thy face and felt thy power;
> Then evil lost its grasp, and passion, hushed,
> Owned the divine enchantment of the hour.
> These were but seasons,—beautiful and rare:
> ABIDE IN ME! and they shall ever be,
> I pray thee now fulfil my earnest prayer:
> Come and ABIDE IN ME, and I in thee."
> — MRS. H. B. STOWE.

"*Work* out your own salvation with fear and trembling. For it is God which *worketh in you* both to will and to do of his good pleasure."—PHILIPPIANS 2: 12, 13.

A VITAL union with the Lord Jesus Christ is essential to all true sanctification. "He that abideth in me, and I in him, the same bringeth forth much fruit: for without me ye can do nothing." All holiness of life that is not the fruit of such a union is mere self-righteousness. It is a specious counterfeit of sanctification. It is the result of self-culture, and, however beautiful it may cause any character to appear to the world, can impart no charm to it in the eye of God.

For the general correctness of their external life, and their scrupulous observance of the divine law, the Pharisees received from men their reward. Their fellow-countrymen honored them as strict religionists. They were charmed as they listened to their long prayers offered at street-corners, or as they beheld their broad phylacteries and ceaseless tithe-paying; but, as these excellences had no connection with the source of all life and power in God,—were not the true expressions of their inward condition, but were to them just as that fruit would be to a tree that was fastened to its branches by outside and artificial ligaments,—so Christ saw nothing to admire in their life, but, on the contrary, expressly declared to His disciples, "That except your righteousness shall exceed the righteousness of the Scribes and Pharisees, ye shall in no case enter into the kingdom of heaven."

The gracious exercise of the soul that is the indispensable *condition* of this union, is *faith*. Detaching us from the first Adam, it unites us to the second. It is this grace which ingrafts us into Christ. Faith brings Jesus into the soul, and makes him who was just now a child of Satan a member of God's household. "But as many as received Him, to them gave He power to become the *sons* of God, even to them that *believe* on His name."

And as faith institutes this union between Christ and the believer, so does it continue it. Jesus abides in the soul no longer than the soul truly believes in Him; and could it not be said of this grace, "and now *abideth* faith," then could we, once in Christ, be afterwards entirely separated from Him. When Paul, speaking of his new life, asserts its origin to be "by the faith of Jesus

Christ," it is to the same cause that he attributes its continuance:—"And the life which I now live in the flesh I live by the faith of the Son of God, who loved me, and gave Himself for me."

The *agency* by which this work is performed is the Holy Spirit. He produces in the soul that grace which is the condition of its union to Christ. Faith is the gift of God. "Except a man be born of water and of *the Spirit*, he cannot enter into the kingdom of God." And, this grace once produced, it is by the same almighty power that it is ever afterwards nourished and maintained. "Grieve not the Holy Spirit of God, whereby ye are sealed unto the day of redemption." "Ye are washed, ye are sanctified, . . . by the Spirit of our God."

The *instrument* employed by the Spirit in the accomplishment of this work is the *truth*. This is the sharp and two-edged sword by which *He* slays the enmity of the human heart to God, and the fire and the hammer by which He breaks to pieces its flinty hardness. "Faith cometh by hearing." It is by the truth that men are led to see that they need conversion. They thus learn how their character appears in the sight of God, what is required of them, and how fearful the consequences must be if they refuse to obey. Indeed, if it is through the instrumentality of motives, *rendered effective by the Spirit*, that the sinner is converted, we cannot conceive how these can lie before the mind and be seen or estimated by it, save in the form of truth. And precisely thus is it with our sanctification. The truth of God is the instrument by which it is accomplished. "Sanctify them through thy truth: thy word is truth."

To the inquiry, then, placed at the head of this chapter, How is sanctification attained? we reply: By the Spirit of God, working through the truth upon a soul that by faith has been vitally united to Christ. It is God's work, not man's.

But does this supersede the necessity of our own personal activity? Because we are sanctified by the Holy Ghost, may we give ourselves up to spiritual indolence? Are we to expect that, irrespective of our own exertions, God will pour into our hearts the grace of sanctification, or fill them with His love, just as summer showers fill lifeless cisterns? When a soul has once yielded itself to Christ, is it true that He, in some unrevealed way and without any of its co-operation, gradually assimilates it to Himself, so that, in full confidence that He will carry on the work to its completion, the Christian may dismiss all trouble about his present imperfect state?

In reply to these inquiries, let this fact be observed. Believers are everywhere in the sacred Scriptures solemnly commanded to grow in grace. They are uniformly addressed as if the work of Christian progress were to be done by themselves alone; and in no case is it intimated that they are under no obligation to advance in holiness unless assisted by some higher influence. "Giving all diligence, add to your faith." "As ye have received of us how ye ought to walk and to please God, so abound more and more." "Be ye perfect, even as your Father which is in heaven is perfect."

Surely it cannot be that our activities are so positively commanded in a work in which we are in fact to be perfectly passive. When God commands men to turn from their sins, or to repent, or to love Him, have they nothing to do? Are they to wait, and make no efforts to obey these divine injunctions, till they are sure that the Holy Spirit is striving with them? The charge brought against the Jews by the prophet was, "They will not frame their doings to turn unto their God." They would not place themselves in such an attitude as to receive the divine assistance. And does not the charge hold with equal force against those who, commanded to abound more and more in all the graces of the Spirit, sit down in idleness, expecting that God will do the work for them?

But, further to show how essential are the believer's own activities in the work of his sanctification, notice what was true, in this particular, of Bible saints.

In the great work of salvation no man ever had a more profound sense of his dependence than Paul. To resist a temptation, to conquer a lust, or to perfect a grace, he knew that his life must link itself, through a Mediator, to God. It was not only wisdom and righteousness that Christ of God was made unto him, but sanctification and redemption. Indeed, looking at Paul's Christian life, we never see him attempting any thing in his own strength. One divine form is ever walking by his side, and one sure and mighty hand is ever leading, blessing, and delivering him.

Yet, at the same time, how intense was his personal activity! Conscious that all his help must come from God, and that he could not take a single step in the divine life without His gracious assistance, he still acted *as if* the whole work was within the circle of his own ability, and *as if* every thing depended upon his own exertions. How remarkable his language! We could not frame words more expressive of strong and personal wrestlings after internal purity: "I keep under my body, and bring it into subjection: lest that by any means, when I have preached to others, I myself should be a cast-away." "Brethren, I count not myself to have apprehended: but this one thing I do, forgetting those things which are behind, and reaching forth unto those things which are before, I press toward the mark

SANCTIFICATION—HOW ATTAINED. 77

for the prize of the high calling of God in Christ Jesus." "I have fought a good fight. I have finished my course. I have kept the faith."

Surely, then, that man's religion is not Pauline who thinks to go on to perfection without personal strugglings and resolves, fastings and prayers. Placing, by faith, his soul in the hands of Christ, "as clay in the hands of the potter, to be moulded by Him into His own heavenly image," Paul had no idea that by this act he absolved himself either from the necessity or duty of working out his own salvation with fear and trembling.

From those modern religious quietists who would teach us such a doctrine, the great Apostle of the Gentiles was at the antipodes. "Let us LABOR," is his language, "to enter into that rest." And with this exhortation how perfectly do the words of Peter—the Apostle of the Circumcision—

agree! "Brethren, *give diligence* to make your calling and election sure."

It would likewise be opposed to all the analogies of life—the figure so generally employed in the sacred Scriptures to illustrate the progress of religion in the soul—to suppose that it had no appropriate *culture*. Every plant, and tree, and animal organism, is indeed dependent for its development upon its own inherent and internal vitality. It grows only because it is possessed of life. And hence, in looking upon any mature development in animated nature,—a stately oak, for example, that for centuries had been in the slow process of growth,—it would be perfectly right to say that it was all but the simple unfolding of its seed's infant life.

> "The pulpy acorn, ere it swells, contains
> The oak's vast branches in its milky veins,
> Each ravelled bud, fine film, and fibre-line,
> Traced with nice pencil on the small design."

But, while this is true, is it not equally true that for the development of either vegetable or animal life, *culture* is indispensable? Will a seed, *though living*, grow, irrespective of its external circumstances? Is it a matter of no moment to the future unfoldings of a grain of wheat whether it finds a home in the soil of some fruitful field where it will enjoy the sunshine and rain of heaven, or is buried in the cerements of some Egyptian mummy?

The essential conditions of growth in nature are, then, clearly two, the existence of life, and its appropriate culture. To secure an abundant harvest, we must first have the buried seed-corn, and then to it must be given air, water, sunlight, wind, and generally the diligent labor of the husbandman.

Thus is it with the life of God in the soul. Though all progress in religion is God's work, and though it may be truly said of sanctification that it is the simple outgrowth of the believer's new life in Christ, yet *culture* is, at the same time, appropriate and necessary to it. It is to be sought by a direct process. There are means for its attainment, providential instruments that foster it, divine helps that favor it, and a method to be employed in order to secure it.

It only remains now that we should inquire what that culture is. And in speaking of *the truth* as the *instrument* of sanctification, we have already indicated the general method. A Christian who would grow in grace must diligently seek to *know* the divine will. He must "buy the truth, and sell it not," "cry after knowledge, and lift up his voice for understanding; seek her as silver, and search for her as for hid treasures."

We often speak, in common language, of the reading of the Bible, prayer, and attendance upon the services and ordinances of God's house, as "means of grace;" and we do so justly. These are the instrumentalities by which the Holy Spirit increases holiness in us, and the fixed channels through which the grace of sanctification flows into our souls. "Thy word," says the Psalmist, "have I hid in mine heart, that I might not sin against thee." "They that wait upon the Lord shall renew their strength." "For my flesh is meat indeed, and my blood is drink indeed."

In the Bible all the graces of the Spirit find their proper aliment. The word feeds *faith* by setting before it the free grace of God, His rich promises and His almighty power to perform them all; *repentance*, by making the vileness and deformity of sin more distinct and impressive; *love*, by opening to our view more and more of the excellence and loveliness of Christ; *hope*, by revealing to us God's abundant compassion and grace; and *zeal*, by that eternal inheritance of glory which it assures us awaits all the faithful in heaven. Of all true sanctification the Bible is the *text-book;* and one might as well expect to become a historian without reading history, as to attain to saintliness of Christian character with God's word neglected.

And the same invigoration of all the graces of the Spirit is accomplished by *prayer*. An affecting commerce between heaven and earth, and the true antitype of that ladder which Jacob saw in the vision of Bethel, prayer, as it ascends to God, brings down from Him both light to understand truth and strength to obey it. And though the petition we offer may in itself include but a single spiritual gift, yet in its answer is contained the increase of all Christian excellences. The prayer, "Lord, increase our faith," strengthens hope and love and patience and zeal, and the whole sisterhood of the Christian graces.

Moreover, in the divine economy prayer is a condition without which God has not promised to bestow a single blessing upon men. How vain, then, the expectation of growing in grace, while the life is prayerless! We can have fellowship with Jesus Christ only as we diligently seek Him.

Of the Church, with its Sabbath services and simple though sublime ordinances, the tendency to produce the same result is obvious. Indeed, what is the Church, but a *house* built for the *new man*, a place in which the peculiar wants of a babe in Christ are especially provided for, where he may be sheltered, watched over, fed, and where, by diligent care, he may, through the grace of God, in time grow up to a vigorous Christian manhood?

In the journey to heaven the Church is to every believer just what the "Palace Beautiful" was to Christian in Bunyan's allegory, "a house built by the Lord of the hill, for the relief and security of pilgrims." It is the home of "Discretion, Prudence, Piety, and Charity," sisters whose discourse is sweet and profitable. It has a "table furnished with fat things, and wine that is well refined." It is full of "rarities; has an armory complete with all manner of furniture, which the Lord has provided for pilgrims." And from it, *"if the day be clear,"* you may even behold the "Delectable Mountains."

CHAPTER VI.

SANCTIFICATION—THROUGH SUFFERING.

> "The heart that God breaks with affliction's rod,
> Oft, like the flower when stricken by the storm,
> Rises from earth, more steadfastly to turn
> Itself to heaven."

"For our light affliction, which is but for a moment, worketh for us a far more exceeding and eternal weight of glory."—2 Cor. 4: 17.

FEW facts are more remarkable or noteworthy in the Bible than the feelings which it commands *Christians* to cherish in the experience of earthly trials. When exposed to severe temptation, persecuted, defamed, beggared in property, or deprived of health and kindred, we are wont to regard the event as calamitous and a just occasion for grief. Philosophy may, indeed, in such circumstances, tell us that the affliction is unavoidable, and bid us dry up our tears, for the reason that they cannot bring back to us our lost comforts; but further than this it never goes. The Stoics taught that a man was wise and advanced towards perfection in proportion as he approached a state of profound apathy. The sum of man's duty with respect to himself was, in their opinion, to subdue his passions of joy, sorrow, hope, and fear. When Servius Sulpicius, the friend of the renowned Cicero, sought to comfort him in the death of his beloved daughter Tullia, he asked, "Is it possible that a mind long exercised in calamities so truly severe should not become totally callous and indifferent to every event?"

How striking the contrast between this teaching of an undevout philosophy and the inspired injunctions of God's word! "My brethren, count it all *joy* when ye fall into divers temptations." "Behold, we count them *happy* which endure." "Blessed is the man whom thou chastenest, O Lord." "Blessed are ye when men shall revile you, and persecute you, and shall say all manner of evil against you falsely, for my sake. *Rejoice*, and be *exceeding glad.*"

That these commands and exhortations are addressed to *true believers only*, and that they refer entirely to those afflictions and trials which God Himself brings upon them, it is of the greatest moment to notice. When men heedlessly run into danger, or purposely bring upon themselves affliction, these blessed passages of inspiration are to them wholly inapplicable. If God chasten us, it is our high privilege "to rejoice," and in doing so we manifest the strength of our confidence in Him; but if our flagellation be, like that of many heathen or Popish devotees, *self-inflicted*, it is the most arrant presumption to suppose that we have any reason for joy.

But the inspired passages already quoted,

while they exhort Christians to *rejoice in tribulation,* indicate in their context the reason for the command: "Knowing this, that the trying of your faith worketh patience. But let patience have her perfect work, that ye may be *perfect* and *entire,* wanting nothing." In the immediate endurance itself of any earthly affliction there cannot, of course, be any element of joy. "Now no chastening for the present seemeth to be joyous, but grievous." The occasion for rejoicing is mainly in its final result: "Nevertheless, afterward it yieldeth the peaceable fruits of righteousness unto them which are exercised thereby."

The sanctification, then, of believers is, under God, promoted by their earthly trials; and this is the reason why in all the sorrows of life they are commanded to rejoice. "Falling tears wash the affections white;" heaving sighs break the power of earthly temptation; bodily pain strengthens our aspirations after heavenly happiness; and out of disappointed hopes, and from sick-beds and funerals, we come with our immortal strength renewed. Indeed, the trials and troubles of this life are but the active ministers of God, ordained and employed by Him to discipline His people into independence of this world and into a ripeness for immortality.

"All sorrow ought to be *home-sickness*," says a German poet. It ought to fill Christ's pilgrim band with longings after rest in His likeness and bosom. And does it not? Should we desire to find an eminent example of piety, would we not say, with the devout McCheyne, "Commend me to a bruised brother, a broken reed, a man of sorrows"? "Is it not upon those jewels that Christ especially esteems, and means to make most resplendent, that He hath His tools oftenest?"

The celebrated master of Rugby, Dr. Arnold, had a sister who was a confirmed invalid for twenty years. Upon her death, he thus portrayed her character, in a letter to Archbishop Whately: "I never saw a more perfect instance of the spirit 'of power and of love and of a sound mind;' intense love, almost to the annihilation of selfishness; a daily martyrdom for twenty years, during which she adhered to her early-formed resolution of never talking about herself; ... enjoying every thing lovely, graceful, beautiful, high-minded, whether in God's works or man's, with the keenest relish; inheriting the earth to the very fulness of the promise, though never leaving her crib nor changing her posture; and preserved through the very valley of the shadow of death from all fear or impatience, or from every cloud of impaired reason which might mar the beauty of Christ's Spirit's glorious work. May God grant that I might come but within one hundred degrees of her place in glory!"

But how is this great work of the believer's sanctification advanced by earthly trials? In the same way, we reply, that all life is made vigorous:—by being measured against competition; by resistance; by standing up against a power that was seeking to destroy it; by wrestling with some antagonistic force. How full of illustrations of this truth is every thing around us! Behold that tree, beneath whose far-reaching shade the flocks repose! It was a law of its being, impressed on the seed, that if left to itself it would steadily unfold its leaves and stretch out its branches. But *such sturdiness* and size it never could have attained in the enjoyment of a quiet and peaceful culture. It was the *fury of storms* that gave it its present gigantic proportions and strength. Every blast of the tempest swaying its boughs loosened the soil in which it stood, and thus suffered its roots to thrust themselves deeper into the earth; while for every new tendril that clasped its tiny fibres around the broken soil, it lifted higher into the air its branches.

The human frame also, when free from disease, will grow to a *certain* fulness and stature. The child of luxury, doomed to a slothful life, may yet have a manly form, but in each muscle and limb there is a mightier energy, which *labor* alone can develop. When compared with the husbandman long inured to toil, or the wrestler who has toughened his sinews by their most vigorous use, he is weak and helpless.

And thus is it even with national life. To become strong and vigorous, the discipline of occasional adversity seems to be essential. A people who, like Moab of old, are "at ease from their youth, remain settled on their lees, and are not emptied from vessel to vessel,"—that is, enjoy unbroken prosperity and are shaken by no great overturnings,—will, like Moab, retaining its old

SANCTIFICATION—THROUGH SUFFERING.

idolatry and barbarity, make no advancement in moral purity and excellence. China, for so many centuries a stranger to internal changes and convulsions, going on in the unbroken enjoyment of a certain kind of national prosperity, has now an effete civilization, and is absolutely hopeless as regards the promise of a regenerated future; "while England, four times conquered and three times deluged with civil war, converted, reformed, and re-reformed, has finally, from all these seeming disasters, emerged, in law, liberty, intelligence, and religion, one of the first and mightiest nations of the world."

The principle is equally applicable in religion. The life of God in the soul, like all other life, is increased by being put forth, and strengthened by resistance. It does not reach its full maturity when nourished alone by prayer, meditation, and the reading of the word. *Suffering*, in some of its many forms, must be introduced.

The soul must have obstacles with which to contend, temptations to resist, and enemies with which to grapple and wrestle itself up into vigor.

But, further to see how the trials of life promote the progress of the believer in holiness, we should observe what a great revealer of *truth*—the *instrument*, let it be remembered, of sanctification—they are. We often marvel that men are so ignorant of themselves. *Savans*, sometimes, in worldly learning, we think it strange that they can voluntarily remain without the least knowledge of self. But in what school is this ignorance so rapidly dissipated as in that of affliction? Joseph's brethren, when feeding upon the abundance of Canaan, did not feel that they were sinners in selling him into bondage. That unnatural crime was in their prosperity forgotten. But when, poor and friendless, they stood in the presence of a foreign king, trembling for their lives, it was remembered; and, despite the long interval between the sin and the sorrow, something constrained them in a moment to link the two together: "We are verily guilty concerning our brother." And how many afflicted souls are constrained to repeat for themselves a similar confession! Between physical suffering and moral evil, men instinctively feel that the connection is indissoluble.

What an impressive teacher, also, of our personal frailty and dependence is affliction!

When a man is in perfect health,—his sinews knit in strength and his nerves all strung harmoniously,—it is a very hard thing for him to believe that "his breath is in his nostrils," that "he is crushed before the moth," and that any moment his earthly tabernacle may be taken down. Indeed, in such statements he has no real faith; and hence all appeals to a religious life founded upon them are almost useless. But let now sickness and sorrow come, and these truths are instantly realized. The man feels that he may be at the very threshold of the eternal Judge; and every motive of self-interest cries aloud to him for preparation.

The pious Rutherford, in a letter to a friend, speaking of some of the ways by which he might grow in grace, says: "Persuade yourself that the King is coming. Read His letter sent before Him, Behold, I come quickly. Wait with the wearied night-watch for the breaking of the eastern sky, and think that you have not a morrow." And with the same considerations did the apostles and early preachers of Christianity frequently exhort their hearers to increased watchfulness. "The end of all things is at hand: be ye therefore sober, and watch unto prayer." "Be ye also patient; . . . for the coming of the Lord draweth nigh." "This I say, brethren, the time is short." But these motives, to what can they appeal when life has been all unclouded sunshine? Can such a man realize that his very next step may be into eternity?

But it is not of ourselves only that the trials of life instruct us. They reveal likewise *the truth* with regard to this world.

When in the enjoyment of an unvaried prosperity men look out upon this world, it oftentimes seems to them almost like a happy island of the blest,—an elysium,—a place upon which the sunshine of heaven rests, and whose inhabitants enjoy perennial bliss. That happiness which their immortal nature demands, they fancy that this earth is able to impart; and, should its wealth or honor be theirs, they think that they would not need to look elsewhere for enjoyment. But how is this spell broken and this delusion dissipated by the incursion of sorrow! "To him whose 'trembling house of clay, languor and disease invade,' what is the whole Pantheon of this world's idols worth?" Can they tranquillize his mind, bribe disease to extract its sting, cause him to forget his pains, or even assure him of ultimate recovery? We concede that "men of sorrow" are in danger of becoming cynical in their views of this world, and may sometimes condemn and disapprove of what ought to be received with thanksgiving; but are they not right when they regard all its pleasures as unsatisfactory and perishable, and those men as foolish who pursue with an all-absorbing interest any mere earthly good?

A distinguished Christian scholar thus speaks of the influence upon his own mind of a severe and long-protracted illness: "Have you ever stood upon the banks of a mighty river, when its swollen waters were passing rapidly by, and watched the bubbles that successively rose and burst upon the agitated surface? They came up and vanished without noise, and to a cursory observer neither their appearance nor disappearance would have been noticed, so numerous were they upon the broad expanse. True, some of them were larger than others; but to an eye that took in the whole surface they all appeared small, nor did the bursting of the largest arrest for a moment the stream that bore them onward. A just emblem, this, of the stream of human society as it appears upon a bed of sickness. Men then perceive that they are but the bubbles on its surface, and that when they disappear the great current will move on unaffected by the change."

But, in addition to this knowledge of ourselves and the world, what a teacher of *the truth* about God is earthly trial! It both impels us to the study of His character, and gives us that disposition of mind without which all study of such a theme would be useless.

When a man feels in any measure his own sinfulness, and realizes the emptiness of this world as the soul's portion,—lessons which, we have just seen, earthly afflictions teach,—it is to God that his thoughts are instantly turned. The great questions that relate to the soul's salvation then burden his spirit and absorb his attention. In God's plan of saving mercy he has then a personal concern, and upon its sufficiency, stability, and blessedness he is constantly meditating. As, when in nature every thing portends a storm, the careful sailor looks anxiously to his vessel and eagerly inquires as to the strength of her timbers and her capacity of endurance,—as at such a time he examines his ship with a particularity and diligence never before exercised,—so it is when God's people find themselves in "manifold temptations" that they are most apt prayerfully to inquire into "the reason of the hope that is in them."

And if for the successful acquisition of divine truth an humble and childlike disposition be necessary, what—apart from the direct influence of the Spirit of God—is better calculated to beget such a feeling than a deep experience of sorrow?

In beautiful harmony with this remark, and in striking confirmation of its truth, is the fact that so many of our best and most thorough theological treatises were written in periods of great trial to the Church. The martyred saints left behind them strong defences for the truth. All Protestants have in their creeds what are called *doctrines of the Reformers;* and this term is used, not to indicate that these holy men of God were the discoverers of these doctrines, but because, driven in the fierce conflicts with Rome to their proof, they placed them upon an immovable basis of Scripture and reason. Such men as Luther, Melanchthon, and Calvin, though living in an age when the weapons both of steel and logic were red with slaughter, were yet giants in the truth; and, much as we are wont in this nineteenth century to boast of our learning, we still frequently go back for wisdom to their writings.

It is also to those English Puritans and Non-Conformists of the seventeenth century, whose homes were in exile or in dungeons, who endured living griefs and "heart-aches ever new," that we are indebted for the most valuable works on practical religion that we now possess. It was then that Flavel uncovered the "Fountain of Life," Alleine sounded the "Alarm," Baxter uttered his thrilling "Call to the Unconverted," Howe discoursed about the "Redeemer's Tears," and Bunyan wrote the "Pilgrim's Progress."

Here, then, are some of the ways in which the believer's sanctification is promoted by his suffering. How happy for us all would an abiding faith in this truth be!—the trials of life God's appointed ministers, His great assayers, to consume all the remains of sin in our heart. Alas that all Christians do not lift themselves up into this sublime confidence! Without it, we are necessarily, in the experience of any earthly affliction, impatient, peevish, restless, unhappy; with it, we can fully obey that divine injunction, "My brethren, count it all joy when ye fall into divers temptations."

> "'*I know,*' is all the mourner saith:
> *Knowledge* by *suffering* entereth,
> And life is perfected by death;
>
> "I am content to touch the brink
> Of pain's dark goblet, and I think
> My bitter drink a wholesome drink.
>
> "I am content to be so weak:
> Put strength into the words I speak,
> For I am strong in what I seek.
>
> "I am content to be so bare
> Before the archers! everywhere
> My wounds being stroked by heavenly air.
>
> "'Glory to God—to God!' he saith:
> *Knowledge by suffering entereth,*
> *And life is perfected by death.*"

CHAPTER VII.

PAUL—AN EXAMPLE OF SANCTIFICATION.

"Plant in me a faith secure and stable
In the work which thou, O God, hast planned,
That no sneers, nor my own doubts, be able
To destroy the faith wherein I stand.
* * * * * *
Like St. Paul's, let this be my endeavor,
That the life I live I may live ever
Through the faith of Him who loved me so."

"Howbeit, for this cause I obtained mercy, that in me first Jesus Christ might show forth all long-suffering, for a *pattern* to them which should hereafter believe on him to life everlasting."—1 TIM. 1: 16.

HAVING in previous chapters examined, with some care, the general subject of the believer's sanctification abstractly, it is natural to expect that we should now seek, by some *forcible examples*, to illustrate it. And many considerations invite to such a course. Men are ordinarily more impressed by what they see embodied in real life than by that which is described to them by mere words. They would study character as they do a fine art, not by the simple statement of formal definitions and rules, but from actual specimens. Thus, the life of Washington is a more impressive teacher of *patriotism*, and that of Napoleon Bonaparte of *ambition*, than the most accurate and exhaustive analysis of either which any pen could write or tongue utter.

In seeking, however, to present to our readers illustrious examples of the believer's sanctification, we at once encounter formidable difficulties. The work is hidden and internal. It is one of the soul; and all men do not
> " bear their hearts
> Nailed on their breasts."

The outward life does not infallibly indicate the soul's real condition. Character and reputation are not always coincident. A religious diary, however conscientiously kept, may still present us with an imperfect and one-sided view of the real man. And of religious biography it is certainly not too much to say that it is often more eulogistic than truthful.

The possibility of mistake is, then, the difficulty that we feel in seeking to deduce our desired illustrations from the pages of uninspired church-history. Examples of sanctification drawn from this source and described as they there appear, we cannot always affirm that in our words there is no shadow of exaggeration.

We have, indeed, no purpose in such a remark to weaken the faith of any in the eminent piety of those men whose memories the Church has enshrined in her deepest affections, nor yet to deter any from both the study and the imitation of their character. Our aim is one very different from the disparagement of these holy men. It is simply to exalt the inspired and the infallible above the uninspired and the fallible, and to lead men for the best illustrations of Christian progress to go to the unerring word of God, rather than to human compositions. As examples of sanctification, *we do well*, it may be, to look at "the judicious Owen," "the seraphic Howe," "the holy Baxter," or, in later times, to such men as Martyn, Neff, Payson, and McCheyne; but certainly *we do better* when Peter, James, John, and Paul are the characters we study. And is it not for the very purpose of enabling us to do this, that the Bible *abounds* in biography?

It is, then, to God's word, and to that alone, that we would look for examples of sanctification. And here, from the many holy men of whom we might speak, we select one, Paul, the great Apostle of the Gentiles; both because of the natural boldness of his character, which made his religious experience vivid and strongly marked, and because so much is said in the sacred Scriptures, not only of his external life, but of his internal and spiritual conflicts.

In looking at Paul's character, what first impresses us is, doubtless, his wonderful activity. We think of him as a *missionary* before we think of him as a *saint*. His external life, so full of almost superhuman labor, it is upon this that we first fix our eye. We remember the journeys he took, the discourses he preached, the voluntary exile from friends that he endured, and the life amid strangers that he lived. Regarding men everywhere as exposed to the wrath of God, Paul sought to go *everywhere*, that to all he might announce the glad tidings of salvation through Christ. But beneath all this outward activity was there not a diligent cultivation of inward piety, a wonderful and constant growth in grace, and a very remarkable subjugation of all the evil passions of the soul?

We propose, in replying to these inquiries, to attempt a somewhat careful analysis of Paul's character at three different epochs in his eventful life.

It is in connection with the martyrdom of Stephen that Saul of Tarsus is first introduced to our notice in the sacred Scriptures. And though a Spanish painter, in a picture of that scene, represents him as walking by the martyr's side with melancholy calmness and with an expression of countenance in striking contrast with the ferocity of the crowd, yet Luke, the inspired historian, gives us a very different impression. Saul was in this persecution an eminent and active agent. He was a distinguished member of that synagogue which, first "disputing" with Stephen and unable to resist his wisdom and spirit, afterwards arraigned him, upon the charge of blasphemy, before the Sanhedrin; and, doubtless, in both the discussion and arraignment he bore a leading part. Moreover, it was "at his feet"—as one peculiarly interested in Stephen's death—that "the witnesses laid down their clothes."

But this single act of persecution was but the first unfolding of Saul's real spirit and temper. Elected—as is generally supposed—a member of the Sanhedrin soon after the martyrdom of Stephen, and possibly as a reward for the active part that he had taken against that heretic, the zeal evinced by him in conducting the persecution was unbounded. He "breathed out threatenings and slaughter against the disciples of Christ;" he was "exceedingly mad against them;" "he made havoc of the church;" he "shut up many of the saints in prison;" he "compelled them to blaspheme." That he might extend the reach of his persecuting power, the sanctuaries of domestic life were invaded. He "entered into every house;" and when in any cases sentence was doubtful, he gave his vote against them. And not only did *men* thus suffer at his hands, but women also,—a fact three times repeated as a great aggravation of his cruelty. He was a "blasphemer, a persecutor, and injurious."

And doubtless it was for the simple purpose of giving to his persecuting spirit a still wider range that, leaving Jerusalem, where the Roman government would not suffer any thing like a systematic destruction of its subjects, he sought to go to Damascus, a city where—it being at that time under the control of Aretas, an Arabian prince— no principles of Roman tolerance would operate as a check on his murderous spite. What a character do these facts exhibit! Was there ever a heart more full of pride and hate, uncharitableness and self-will? How pitiless the man! how relentless, how unsparing! He was the prince of Inquisitors.

But such the character of Saul, the proud

Jewish Pharisee, when converted by the vision and the voice of Christ, on the way to Damascus, into Paul the Apostle; behold him at another and subsequent epoch in his life.

After twenty years of the most consuming toil in the propagation of Christianity, and after suffering in his work every thing but death, sad tidings reached the apostle, with reference to one of the churches planted by his ministry. At Corinth, as in other places, emissaries had arrived from the Judaizers of Palestine; and as, in a community so civilized and refined, every attempt to insist upon circumcision would have been vain, they commenced a personal attack upon the apostle. They denied his apostleship, charged him with selfish and mercenary motives, accused him of egregious vanity, ridiculed his "bodily presence," and affirmed that he was as vacillating in his teaching as in his practice. And the endeavors of these agitators to undermine Paul's influence were to a great extent successful. Many of his own children in the faith had their confidence in him and their love towards him greatly lessened.

And then, too, of those who were still steadfast to the doctrines of the apostle, not a few, preferring the Alexandrian learning with which Apollos had enforced his preaching to the simple and unadorned style of Paul, called themselves by his name, and looked with some measure of coldness upon their first teacher.

How exceedingly trying such intelligence! And in the manner in which it is received what a revelation of character must necessarily be made! Its appeal is to the very strongest passions of human nature, to those which master the highest and noblest men, and which are the very last in any bosom to be successfully resisted. Its voice is to ambition, jealousy, and pride. And to such a man as Paul will it speak in vain? Think of him just as a moment since we sketched his character,—as Saul the persecutor,—and would he have quietly borne such treatment? Would he have suffered himself to be so defamed? Would he have had no jealous feelings towards the eloquent Apollos, and no wounded pride at finding that his fame was fast being eclipsed? We cannot doubt what Saul of Tarsus would have felt and said in such circumstances.

But Paul the Apostle, how different! Read his two epistles to this Church, written in view of the facts just referred to, and you will not find in them all one word of disappointed ambition, corroding jealousy, or wounded pride. Indeed, these passions —always of great strength in the unsanctified heart, and of peculiar power in Paul's natural disposition—seem now, by the grace of God, to have been perfectly subdued. His proud and passionate nature transformed by the divine Spirit, Paul, under these severest provocations, could, with David, say, "Surely I have behaved and quieted myself as a child that is weaned of his mother: my soul is even as a weaned child."

Had Paul any *ambition* to become a leader of a party in Corinth, and to make for himself a name? Did he feel that chagrin so natural to all men upon learning that his personal influence was declining among his old friends? Not at all. His individuality was entirely merged in the great cause he advocated. "Who then is Paul, and who is Apollos, but ministers by whom ye believed? . . . So then neither is he that planteth any thing, neither he that watereth."

Of the constantly waxing power of Apollos, and of the frequent unfavorable comparisons made between him and the eloquent pupil of Alexandria, was Paul jealous? The fact that the affections of his converts were beginning to be transferred from him—an apostle—to an inferior, did it ruffle for a moment his tranquillity? Observe his affectionate language in speaking of his rival, and his earnest desire that the Corinthian Church might again enjoy his labors: "As touching our *brother* Apollos, I greatly desired him to come unto you with the brethren."

And, though charged with bigotry, avarice, and moral cowardice, though "his presence" was said "to be weak, and his speech contemptible," was his pride offended, and did he either shut himself up in dignified silence, or with violent words condemn such ingratitude? Surely, "if pride were ever venial, it had been here." But in vain will you look in either of his epistles for the least manifestation of it. On the contrary, so great was his humility as to solicit from these very Corinthians a renewal of the love which had grown so cold: "Behold, this third time I am ready to come to you. . . . And I will very gladly spend and be spent for you, though the more abundantly I love you, the less I be loved."

That a conscientious sense of duty constrained the apostle to utter against his wayward and erring brethren at Corinth many terrible denunciations, is indeed true; but how striking the contrast between the *spirit* in which these were uttered, and that evinced by him at an earlier period of his life! To Saul, the punishment of suspected heretics seemed to be a delight; but to Paul, it was a strange work. The grace of God had changed the whole spirit of the persecutor. "Crucified with Christ," Paul had now put on His meekness and gentleness. His very threatenings were full of love. He grieved over the obstinacy of his opponents, and his own heart was pained by the denunciations that he was constrained to utter against others. How strange to read, from the very pen that once rejoiced to write the sentence of death against the disciples of Christ, such a sad lament as this over the necessity of administering stern rebukes to the erring! "For if I make you sorry, who is he that maketh me glad?"

But we pass from this second epoch in Paul's life to a third.

After ten years more of toil and sacrifice for Christ, Paul is a prisoner at Rome. He had been in like circumstances before; but now, either because of the peculiar severity of Nero's character, or from the nature of the accusations brought against him, his imprisonment was more severe. He was not only chained, as before, to his military guard, but treated "as a malefactor." The privilege of preaching the gospel, enjoyed in his first imprisonment, was now denied him. Friends visited him in his confinement rarely, and only with the greatest difficulty; and to show any public sympathy with him was so perilous that in the first stage of his trial no Christian ventured to attend him. Nor was this sad prison-life of the apostle cheered by any hope of final acquittal. On the contrary, every thing assured him that it would terminate in his death. He saw continually before him, and at a very little distance, the doom of an unrighteous magistrate, and the glittering sword of a Roman executioner. And with what feelings? Did Paul complain that his lot was a hard one? Was he unsubmissive? A life so full of toil for Jesus, did the apostle feel that his death should have been peaceful, and that Elijah's chariot and horses were more his due than a bloody martyrdom? The very reverse was true.

According to the best Biblical chronologists, it was mid-summer when Paul was led out from his prison in Rome to the place of execution, and but a few months previous —in the early spring—that he wrote in his second epistle to Timothy, his well-beloved son in the Lord, that sublime strain of triumphant hope familiar to the memory of every Christian: "I have fought a good fight, I have finished my course, I have kept the faith: henceforth there is laid up for me a crown of righteousness, which the Lord, the righteous judge, shall give me at that day." What saintliness is here! What ripeness of character for heaven! How remarkable the vision of a man, still an inhabitant of earth, yet, in all his affections and aspirations, so thoroughly in the world to come!

CHAPTER VIII.

PAUL'S SANCTIFICATION — THE METHOD OF ITS ATTAINMENT.

"Brethren, I count not myself to have apprehended: but this one thing I do, forgetting those things which are behind, and reaching forth unto those things which are before, I press toward the mark for the prize of the high calling of God in Christ Jesus."—PHIL. 3: 13, 14.

NO Christian can look at the character of Paul, as just described, without feeling a deep interest in the inquiry, How did the apostle attain to so remarkable a measure of personal sanctification? Beholding him on "the highway of holiness" so much in advance of other travellers,—on a mountain crowned with the richest verdure and bathed in the sunlight of Heaven, while the great majority of God's people linger in the dark and barren valley below,—every pious soul is filled with the lofty ambition of emulating his virtues and following in his footsteps. True, the standard is so lofty, and so far removed from ordinary life, that imitation seems almost impossible. We crave a lower ideal after which to pattern our character. But, as inspiration says of the prayers of that old prophet which were so effectual,—" Elias was a man subject to like passions as we are,"—so may we not say of Paul's sanctification? Had he any religious capacities which we do not possess?

Nothing is more evident than that the apostle regarded his conduct and character as imitable; for to their imitation he was constantly exhorting all his brethren. Indeed, there is scarcely a letter written by Paul to any of the Churches in which, while he presents Christ as the *only* perfect example of holy living, the *only ultimate* pattern, he does not likewise speak of himself as to the same end *intermediate and secondary*. "I beseech you, be ye followers of me." "I would that all men were even as I myself." "Brethren, be ye followers of me, and mark them which walk as ye have us for an ensample." "Those things which ye have both learned, and received, and heard, and *seen in me,* do."

The question we propose to consider is, then, wholly practical. The path in which Paul walked, we may walk; and that measure of holiness which he attained, it is our privilege to secure.

Now, bearing this fact in mind, and cherishing all the interest that it is so well calculated to awaken, we proceed at once to the inquiry, How did Paul become so Christ-like? What made him so pre-eminent for his piety? How did *he live,* in character to approach so near to a perfect standard? Was his holiness the result of any direct divine communications, that is, communications made to him irrespective of his own activity? Were there mystical openings in his soul, through which God poured the grace of sanctification? Had Paul a constitutional predisposition to piety? or was it all the casual result of external circumstances? We have already seen that this is not the way in which men become holy. Progress in religion, like advancement in every thing else, is subject to law. It is reducible to order, and has its fixed conditions. It is conformed, just like any other accomplishment of life, to regular method. And Paul was holy simply because he sought to be holy in the way God appointed for securing it.

What that way is, the passage from one of his epistles, placed at the beginning of this chapter, is a full exposition. In it Paul reveals to us the secret of his holiness. He uncovers to our view his internal and spiritual history. He tells us what were his views of himself and his purposes of life, and so definitely marks every step in his progress in holiness that no one can fail instantly to perceive them: "Brethren, I count not myself to have apprehended: but this one thing I do, forgetting those things which are behind, and reaching forth unto those things which are before, I press toward the mark for the prize of the high calling of God in Christ Jesus."

Paul here mentions five things which may be regarded as the means employed by him for the attainment of holiness; or, rather, as the great principles which, governing his life, resulted, by the divine blessing, in his eminent piety.

1. Paul never thought himself perfect, never regarded his Christian life as complete: "*Brethren, I count not myself to have apprehended.*"

At his miraculous conversion when on the way to Damascus, his justification—through faith in the sacrifice and work of Christ—

perfect and complete, his sanctification, Paul felt, was but initial, and was to continue through life progressive. Instead of resting upon the simple fact of his regeneration as sealing his soul infallibly for heaven, he regarded this as only the beginning of a new life, to be assiduously cultivated, a piece of "solid moral masonry to be carried on and up by a lifelong toil." Conscious that there still remained in his heart very much of ingratitude, ignorance, and lust, and that it was the aim of Christianity to remove them altogether, he felt that each passing day, bearing its part in this work, should bring to him an intenser glow of love, and a wider horizon of knowledge, and a more perfect subjugation of passion.

When Paul first entered upon his religious life, it is natural to suppose that some particular *sin* may in a very special degree have troubled him. Thus, by nature of a fierce and almost ungovernable temper, it is quite likely that at first he was irascible and peevish, and that to conquer this he had to direct all his energies. But, a victory at this point achieved, was he satisfied? "I count not myself," is his language, "to have apprehended." His eclaircised vision saw at once other evils to be subdued and other bosom-sins to be eradicated; and to this he instantly set to work. That pleasing delusion which sometimes steals over men, and which leads them to sit down satisfied with themselves, and to feel that they are already perfect, never found a place in the bosom of the great Apostle of the Gentiles. His introspection was too keen ever to allow him to boast of a spotless purity.

And here lies the foundation of all effort to secure holiness, *the profound conviction of its need.* Spiritual pride is an axe at the very root of all Christian progress. A Laodicean professor—a man in his own esteem "rich and increased with goods, and needing nothing"—can never be holy. Just as a feeling of ignorance leads to the acquisition of knowledge, or a consciousness of disease prompts an application to a physician, does a deep realization of moral imperfection lead to the cultivation of holiness.

2. But, while Paul was thus continually conscious that as yet his character was imperfect, he was equally constant in his determination that it should not remain so; and to the accomplishment of this purpose he gave the undivided energies of his soul. Perfection was the goal of his life. The acquisition of personal holiness was the single aim of his existence. "*This one thing I do.*"

Upon the mitre of the Jewish high-priest—that part of his sacred investiture which was over and above all the rest, that surmounted the robe, ephod, girdle, and Urim and Thummim—was inscribed, "*Holi-*

ness to the Lord." A like elevation above all earthly purposes and plans did Paul give to his desire after perfection. He coveted the divine favor more than human approbation. To kneel in penitence at the foot of the cross was to him a higher honor than to be introduced to a court of fashion; and the secret whisperings of the Spirit he regarded as dearer possessions than certificates of office or inventories of wealth. In a word, every thing was made by the apostle to converge, either directly or indirectly, towards his soul's sanctification. His whole existence was a *unit.* One single purpose pervaded it all.

And thus must it be with those who, like this great apostle, would perfect holiness in the fear of the Lord. Men never attain to any high measure of sanctification, to quote another's language, "by a few desultory snatches of sober reflection, or a few vague impressions in churches or graveyards.

Holiness, to be secured, must be treated as an interest, a pursuit, a profession. It must be made the *vocation* of the soul, the business of life, the practical handicraft of the inner man. It must be begun, continued, and never ended. The Bible must be its text-book, prayer its rehearsal, and all the circling hours of time the periods of its exercise." To become holy, men must set before themselves a perfect standard of excellence and ceaselessly struggle to shape their lives to it. They must not be self-indulgent when they ought to be self-denying, tolerant of imperfections that it is their duty to eradicate, and asleep over faults of character which should awaken godly jealousy.

But, amid all the turmoil and vexing cares of secular business, is this possible? Can a man who is necessarily absorbed in a worldly avocation say, with Paul, "This one thing I do"? Can he make the attainment of personal holiness the great aim and purpose of his life? In the case of a minister we can easily see how the example of the apostle may be followed. Every thing he is called to do seems naturally to promote his sanctification. But is it so with men of the world and business? Must we not have for them a different and a somewhat lower principle of action? Not at all, we reply. For "holiness is not *doing*, but *being*." It is not to effect an act, but to achieve a character. It is to become Christ-like; and every moment of life, and every act of life, is an opportunity for securing this.

A man cannot pray—that is, directly and formally—and yet labor. The latter must be intermitted when the former is performed. But a man may all the time be growing holy, at his home and in his shop, while conversing with his friends or trafficking in articles of trade, as well as when in church worshipping God. Ay, more in the former places than in the latter; for it is the very temptations to anger, evil-speaking, pride, and dishonesty, which at home and in the shop are most apt to rise, that furnish us with the opportunities of mastering ourselves and becoming Christ-like. Luther uttered a truthful sentiment when he said,

> "Not more devout the priest can be
> Than Christian housemaid with her broom
> Her work pursuing faithfully."

3. But another important principle in Paul's method of attaining holiness is seen in his *treatment of the past.* Read again his inspired words: "Brethren, I count not myself to have apprehended," I never feel as if I had reached the goal of my Christian life, *perfection*:—"but this one thing I do,"—my fixed determination is finally to attain it,—"*forgetting those things which are behind,* and reaching forth unto those things which are before."

Not a few of the professed disciples of

Christ are continually looking back, to see what they have done for their Master, or what they have left undone. Their position is at the stern of the ship, and their glance is directed towards the wake of the vessel. And in this retrospect do they behold many years of labor in the Church? then, with regard to actual toil in the future, how prone are they to say, "I pray thee, have me excused," "Let some of these young brethren, who have not like me borne the burden and heat of the day, do the work"! Or, on the other hand, does the retrospect show nothing but idleness and guilt? then their remembrance of by-gone faults paralyzes all their energies for future toil.

But no such regard for the past had the Apostle Paul. The fact that he had spent years in the most laborious service for Christ was nothing to him; nor, save to repent of them, did he ever recall the follies of which he had been guilty. Had he been remiss in past duties? Had he allowed some golden opportunities for glorifying God to pass unimproved? Or had he even fallen into some grievous sin? What then? Was it not irreparable? Could tears efface it from the memory of God? Was there any utility in forever brooding over it?

> "Not backward were his glances bent,
> But onward to his Father's home."

"This one thing I do, forgetting those things which are behind."

And this principle, as a means of sanctification, is most potent. To recall past excellences and labors is to engender spiritual pride; to remember past defects and sins is to discourage and dishearten. Should a scholar forever think of what he had accomplished in the world of letters, or of what he might have accomplished had he practised a becoming diligence, he would evidently be at a perfect stand-still in learning. And it is not otherwise with us in our efforts to secure holiness. In the Christian race, men, to be successful, need every thing that is hopeful and stimulating. Their faith should be sanguine, cheerful, active, neither weighted down by the sad memories of an irretrievable past, nor having the loftiness of its aspirations lowered by the remembrance of attainments in piety already made.

4. But, further, to discover how Paul secured for himself so remarkable a degree of personal holiness, we must not fail to observe the motives that stimulated him, or, rather, the goal towards which he ran. Let his inspired words be once more recalled: "Brethren, I count not myself to have apprehended: but this one thing I do, forgetting those things which are behind, and reaching forth unto those things which are before, *I press toward the mark for the prize of the high calling of God.*"

Biblical critics have sometimes made a

distinction between what Paul here designed to denote by the words "*mark*" and "*prize*." They suppose that the first refers to *perfection of character*, and the last to the *blessedness of heaven*. The distinction is not fanciful; neither is the order in which these words occur, undesigned. *Perfection* is placed first, because this was the great motive that stimulated the apostle. He pressed towards "the mark." He earnestly desired to be holy. He sought goodness for its own sake. He followed after piety just as a true scholar follows after knowledge, because it is something to be desired in itself.

But, then, blended with this motive, and doubtless even in his inspired mind inseparable from it, was the personal reward of holiness, that *prize* of blessedness which God has promised to all the faithful.

Moreover, these two things—Christian perfection and Christian blessedness—are here in the same phrase united, because they are in fact inseparable, or, in other words, because the latter is always graduated by the former. "*The prize*" that God holds up to the eye of the believer, and by which He would quicken his laggard steps in the divine life, is not a fixed and definite thing, incapable of addition and unsusceptible to diminution, but, on the contrary, is always proportioned by the degree of progress that we here make towards "*the mark.*"

And precisely thus should it be with us if our aspirations are to walk as close with God as did Paul. We should think *first* of "the mark." Our highest ambition should be a perfect Christian character. We should desire to be holy, not *primarily* because without holiness eternal happiness is impossible, but because our Father which is in heaven is holy. Our religion should not be a mere self-seeking. Indeed, if it is, we are only preparing for ourselves a certain disappointment. But then, after this, and in the intensity of our desire always *second* to this, we should think of "*the prize.*" We should keep steadily before us the thought of home, realize its blessedness, and let the radiant diadem of glory which there awaits us give new vigor to our flagging steps.

How truthful and beautiful is that hymn of the Jesuit Xavier!

> "My God, I love thee, not because
>   I hope for heaven thereby,
> Nor because they who love thee not
>   Must burn eternally.
>
> "Thou, O my Jesus, thou didst me
>   Upon the cross embrace,—
> For me didst bear the nails and spear,
>   And manifold disgrace.

*   *   *   *   *   *

> "Then why, O blessed Jesus Christ,
>   Shall I not love thee well,
> Not for the sake of winning heaven,
>   Or of escaping hell,—
>
> "Nor with the hope of gaining aught,
>   Nor seeking a reward,
> But as thyself hast loved me,
>   O ever-loving Lord?"

5. But one thought more remains; and it is the highest and best of all. Every attempt of Paul to grow in grace was made in humble dependence upon Christ. Read again his own history of his religious life: "Brethren, I count not myself to have apprehended; but this one thing I do, forgetting those things which are behind, and reaching forth unto those things which are before, I press toward the mark for the prize of the high calling of God IN CHRIST JESUS."

Paul believed in a real, personal, ever-living Saviour, and was continually conscious of His presence. That Redeemer who died for his soul's salvation, he believed knew its weakness, visited it in its dangers, comforted it in its sorrows, and chastened it in its wilfulness. He had faith not in a dead Christ *only*, but in a living one also. He felt his whole being encircled and touched with a celestial presence. Another will than his own had begun to work within his own, both to will and to do. He realized that the grand peculiarity of the gospel is that it does not stop with telling men how to act, but enters into their souls by the living person of the Lord, and becomes there an indwelling force, by which they act.

And there is no principle so wondrously efficient for the production of holiness as this. "Christ uttered no syllables more full of tenderness than when He besought His followers to feel that 'without Him they could do nothing;' and never furnished man with an uplifting or propelling impulse so august and benignant as when He said: 'Lo, I am with you alway.'" It is this which brings down the help of the Almighty to renew from day to day the weakness of His children, and it is in proportion to a Christian's faith in this truth that he can do all things.

And it is because we so often forget this dependence, and strive in our own strength to be holy, that we remain so sinful. We fall in the hour of temptation, as Peter sank in the waters of Gennesareth, until, conscious that all our help must come from Christ, we exclaim, as did the sinking apostle, "Lord, save me"!

CHAPTER IX.

THE GREAT MOTIVE TO SANCTIFICATION.

>"Bend with thy fires our stubborn will,
>And quicken what the world would chill,
>And homeward call the feet that stray;
>Virtue's reward and final grace,
>The Eternal Vision face to face,—
>Spirit of Love! for these we pray."
>
>FABER.

"This is the will of God, even your sanctification."— 1 THESS. 4: 3.

THE will of God is the motive of greatest potency to every renewed mind. Fully satisfy a true Christian that any line of conduct you propose for his adoption will meet with the divine approbation, and you cannot but be successful. To the power of this consideration all questions of worldly expediency are secondary. As the soul born of the Spirit looks out upon its history, both in this world and in that which is to come, it is able to exclaim, —just as did Christ in the survey of His mortal career, from the stable where the shepherds found Him, to the sepulchre where the Arimathean laid Him: "Lo, I come! in the volume of the book it is written of me, I delight to do thy will, O my God." Our blessed Saviour said, "My meat is to do the will of Him that sent me;" and again, "For I came down from heaven, not to do mine own will, but the will of Him that sent me;" and "the same mind that was in Christ" is in all His people.

Indeed, where *self-will,* or a disposition to exalt our own preferences and arrangements above those of the Creator, is supreme, there can be no piety. The very essence of true religion is submission. "To do the will of God" is to be adopted into the family of God;* and to "be *complete in all the* will of

---

* Mark 3: 35.

God"—the prayer of Epaphras for the Colossians—is that they might attain to perfection in the divine life.

With regard to the reception of truth by the intellect, Christianity admits of some diversity. Men to be truly the children of God need not have precisely the same doctrinal views. There is no creed that we can carry with us into the universal Church, and to which we can demand subscription as essential to piety. But this is not so with reference to the *will*. In this department of our mental constitution, Christianity admits of no diversity. No man can be a true follower of Christ whose will does not bow in joyful submission to the will of God, and who does not make the divine law the ultimate rule of his life. "Thy *will be done*," is not the shibboleth of a school, but the language of the universal Church. The whole elect of God, in every age and nation, have felt the submission that these words express.

As a religious quietist, Madame Guyon may have but little of our sympathy; but a woman in prison for righteousness' sake, who could thus sing of her joyful submission to the divine will, we cannot but take to our hearts as a true child of God:

> "A little bird I am,
>   Shut from the fields of air;
> And in my cage I sit, and sing
>   To Him who placed me there,
> Well pleased a prisoner to be,
> Because, my God, it pleases thee."

In proposing, then, the inquiry with reference to the believer's sanctification,— What is the will of God? let it not be forgotten that our inquiry regards the motive of greatest potency to every pious mind.

And here how direct and positive is the answer of inspiration! In this world we are oftentimes in doubt with regard to what the divine will is. Some line of conduct suggested to us, and the question with reference to it earnestly asked, "Lord, what wilt thou have me to do?" we still hear no certain and authoritative reply. But it is not so in the case before us: "THIS IS THE WILL OF GOD, EVEN YOUR SANCTIFICATION." God desires that all His people should be holy. Vessels of an invisible sanctuary and emptied of all impurity, He earnestly desires that they should be filled with all that is pure, holy, and beneficent. This is uniformly represented in the Sacred Scriptures as the ultimate end of Christ's sacrifice in our behalf: "He gave himself for us, that He might redeem us from *all* iniquity." And to the accomplishment of this purpose were all the prayers and labors of the inspired apostles directed: "And I pray God your whole spirit and soul and body be preserved blameless unto the coming of our Lord Jesus Christ."

And *sanctification*, the will of God with reference to His people, is also His will in regard to the whole universe. He has consecrated it all for His use; He has devoted it to His service and glory. It is altogether one vast temple, intended solely for purposes of worship and designed to be everywhere vocal with His praise. "The Lord hath made all things for Himself."

But this will of God *universal* is also—if we may so speak—*all-inclusive*. Mark the full force of His declaration. God does not say that He simply desires His people's sanctification,—that this is *one* among the many purposes which He cherishes for them,—but He speaks as if He had no other will but this with reference to them, or as if in this was summed up all that He required of them: "*This is the will of God, even your sanctification.*"

To this view is it objected that other things are spoken of in the Bible as the will of God with reference to His people? It only requires that we should examine these, to find that they all terminate in this one, *their sanctification.* Thus, is God's will said to be His own glory, or, rather, that He should be glorified by His creatures. How can men accomplish this, save as, in moral character like God, or, in other words, *sanctified,* they shadow forth in their lives that divine resemblance? "Herein is my Father glorified, that ye bear much fruit."

"When in summer we behold the earth clothed with luxuriant vegetation, adorned with flowers and enlivened by myriads of sportive, happy beings, and remember that the *sun* is instrumentally the cause of all this, it may in one sense be said to be *glorified* in the earth." In a similar way is Christ, the great Sun of righteousness, glorified by His people. It is when men see sinful and guilty worms of the dust transformed into every thing that in character is beautiful and lovely, and remember that the transformation was wrought by the power of God, that He is in them glorified.

To say, then, that God's will is that "He should be glorified by us," is precisely the same as to say that "His will is our sanctification." The last is the only way by which the former can be accomplished.

But, again, does God require of us to believe in Him? Is the exercise of faith God's will in reference to us? What is sanctification, but the *tree* of which faith is the *root*, or the *end* of that divine life of which faith is the *beginning?* A true belief in Christ, and personal holiness, are not two things distinct from each other and capable of being set over against each other, but, on the contrary, the same thing, at different periods of its existence. The first is the blade, the last the full corn; the first is the tender babe in Christ, the last the strong man. Indeed, the two words are so far synonyms as mutually to imply each other. God desires our faith when He desires our sanctification; and when He wishes us to be holy, He wishes us to believe on Him whom He has sent.

And the same is true of our happiness. Is it said that the will of God is the highest happiness of His creatures? This is but another way of saying that His will is their sanctification. The one necessarily includes the other. Holiness and happiness are linked together as indissolubly as are misery and sin. No man can have "a continual feast" who is inwardly impure; nor can he be a stranger to true happiness on whose soul God has imprinted the image of Himself.

But, the sanctification of His people being the universal and all-inclusive will of God, it is likewise towards its accomplishment that all human events tend. It could not be otherwise. Nothing required for the perfection of His chosen ones will be withheld. God desires their sanctification at any price. The inanimate creation called into existence for the sake of spiritual beings has all its arrangements ordered so as to promote their welfare. It is for the enlargement and strengthening of the Church that all the empires of the world have their rise, history, and decay. For this God changes their laws, alters their boundaries, desolates them by war, or blesses them with peace. Indeed, it is only as the theatre upon which moral beings may develop their character and ripen for heaven, that the whole material system is upheld. It is nothing but a scaffolding to an invisible temple rising within. And when that shall have been completed, and all the moral beings for whom God made the world shall have lived upon it and passed away, the power that now holds it on its poise will be withdrawn, and all its wondrous mechanism will sink into forgetfulness.

And the same is true of the individual believer. The will of God being his sanctification, all the manifold events of life are designed for its accomplishment. To promote our holiness, God gives us in profusion earthly blessings. Tokens of His goodness are showered upon us, that we might be drawn to repentance. And for the same reason God takes away what He had bestowed. He raises the storm in the most serene and brilliant sky, and makes calamity burst forth in the midst of overflowing prosperity.

And this fact, how full of encouragement is it to every pious soul longing for a *closer walk* with God! What you desire for yourself, God desires in your behalf. Indeed, this is the first, last, and only will of God regarding you. It is a desire as strong as yours is weak. It existed long before the first thought of holiness arose in your mind, and was, in fact, its author. It can never abate in its intensity. God now desiring your sanctification must always desire it. And what He wills to accomplish, He has the requisite power to perform. Take courage, then, disciple of Christ: those spiritual foes which would impede your progress in the divine life, though numerous and strong, are not so mighty as the Champion you have found. In striving to be holy, you are not acting alone, but in concert with the great God.

CHAPTER X.

CONNECTION BETWEEN HOLINESS AND USEFULNESS.

> "He that will work for others' good
> Must be HIMSELF renewed:
> So, before all things, thou must try
> THYSELF TO PURIFY."
> —THOLUCK.

"Restore unto me the joy of thy salvation; and uphold me with thy free spirit. *Then* will I teach transgressors thy ways; and sinners shall be converted unto thee."—PSALM 51: 12, 13.

AN earnest desire to extend the triumphs of Christianity is an invariable result of its reception. The unsophisticated promptings of the new-born soul are always to active effort for God. Its very first impulse is that *something must be done.* What it has received, it would communicate. Having been enlightened, it would shine. Its own spiritual thirst satisfied by coming to Christ and drinking of the "living water," it would itself become, as it were, a secondary fountain for quenching the thirst of others.*

Nor is this a mere transient emotion, the gushing forth of a gratitude that will soon spend itself. On the contrary, it is a permanent condition of the soul, or rather it is a desire that time only increases. It was many years after Paul's conversion—twenty, at least—that he said of his countrymen, "My heart's desire and prayer to God for Israel is, that they might be saved." "For I could wish that myself were accursed from Christ for my brethren, my kinsmen according to the flesh." When that eminent Christian Thomas Cranfield was eighty years of age, instead of having his zeal for the conversion of men lessened, it was so greatly increased as to lead him for the enlargement of his usefulness to devise new schemes.

---

* John 7: 37, 38.

Short and pithy Scriptural sentences, written upon slips of paper, and calculated to arouse or edify, were distributed in all his walks.

But for the accomplishment of this desire, universal to believers, what is the highest preparation? As elements of usefulness, any attempt to disparage learning, wealth, or social position would be vain. There is great power for good in them; and when to such an end they are desired, men do well to "covet them earnestly." *"Yet show I unto you a more excellent way." To do good, men should be good. Holiness is the most certain road to usefulness.*

How many Scripture facts and inspired declarations illustrate this truth! That prayer of Christ in behalf of His disciples, "Sanctify them through thy truth," was doubtless offered with reference to their usefulness in the peculiar position in which they were soon to be placed. Our blessed Lord was on the very eve of His crucifixion. A few hours more, and the traitorous kiss, arrest, trial, death, would come. The foundations of the Church, He was about to lay in blood, and then, ascending to His heavenly Father, the great work of building with lively stones, upon this foundation, a spiritual temple, was to be left to His disciples. And now, "O Father, sanctify them," is His prayer; make them holy, take away from them every sin, that they may be qualified for their great work. With what a peculiar beauty and power do these words of Christ teach the connection between holiness and usefulness!

How beautiful, also, is the picture that inspiration presents of the churches in Macedonia! Of one of them Paul says, "For from you sounded out the word of the Lord not only in Macedonia and Achaia, but also in every place your faith to Godward is spread abroad;" and of all, though in "deep poverty" and in "a great trial of affliction," the same apostle testifies that their liberality to the saints at Jerusalem was both beyond his expectation and beyond what in their condition he would have thought possible.

And of this remarkable devotedness Paul gives us the secret in the words, "*They gave their very selves to the Lord first.*"* The Macedonian converts were doubtless true believers before this. They had fled for refuge to the hope set before them. But from this small beginning of piety they had been going on towards perfection. The work of grace had been greatly deepened in their hearts. They had made an entire consecration of themselves to God; and hence their liberality and widely extended influence.

And to these Scriptural illustrations of the connection between holiness and usefulness we would only add the express declaration of Peter, "For if these things be in you

---

* The literal rendering of 2 Cor. 8: 5.

and abound,"—that is, if to faith as a foundation you add all the other graces of Christianity, virtue, knowledge, temperance, patience, godliness, brotherly-kindness, charity, —" they make you that ye shall neither be barren [*idle*] nor unfruitful in the knowledge of our Lord Jesus Christ."

But, further to see how those who would be useful must be holy, observe the fact that almost *all the motives which impel to Christian activity are directly and vitally connected with the soul's internal state.*

One of these is the conviction of the lost condition of men. Christians labor to save men because of their deep and abiding faith in the great truth that they are sinners, and as such exposed to the wrath of God. It is not enough to look upon our race as intellectually and socially degraded, or as robbed of their true dignity and prerogatives. In this aspect of man we have no sufficient basis for such an enterprise as is necessary for his salvation. The spirit that can embrace and sustain a work calling for so much labor and sacrifice as this, can have its origin in no lower view of man than that which recognizes him as morally depraved, and as passing every hour unblessed to his final home.

But to this truth men are sensible just in the proportion of their piety. It is indeed an easy thing for men to hold on this point an orthodox creed; but really to *believe* and *feel* that all are by nature ruined, and can be saved only through Christ's death, requires a large measure of His Spirit. And just as that Spirit is attained are our sensibilities to this truth increased, and our activities quickened.

And the same is true of that high and commanding motive to Christian activity which includes every other, and without which all others would be valueless. We mean the *love of Christ*. First, *His love for us*, shining out from the cross, and beaming down upon us from His mediatorial throne in heaven; secondly, *our love for Him*, a responsive affection enkindled in every renewed heart by the consciousness of His goodness. It was this that "constrained" Paul to "preach among the Gentiles the unsearchable riches of Christ," and that has ever since apostolic times raised up faithful witnesses for the truth. Here lies the germ of all missionary enterprises. It is this that carried the gospel from Jerusalem to every part of the Roman empire, and that is now causing it to be preached in distant and barbarous climes. As Isaac Taylor says of Whitefield, so may we say of all the faithful heralds of salvation : "His motive was not a congeries of reasons and considerations : it was an impulse, spontaneous, irresistible, bright, and fraught with love, hope, and a sure anticipation of abundant success." The love of Christ constrained him.

But this motive to Christian activity, is it any thing more than another name for piety? Our love to Christ, or the consciousness of His love for us, are they not in exact proportion to our growth in grace? Can we conceive of any progress in religion that does not involve an increase of love? Can we take one step towards heaven without having in our esteem "the exceeding riches of His grace" magnified, and without having our affection for Him, in turn, quickened and enlarged?

But, leaving here the *motives* that impel believers to labor for Christ, how impressively are we taught the connection between holiness and usefulness, by observing the *agencies* for doing good, that Christians may employ; and the obvious fact that these are all mainly dependent for their efficiency upon the personal holiness of those who use them!

In speaking of the *means* that God has put into the hands of the Church for evangelism, we are wont to give the first place to *prayer.* And this is right. Prayer lies at the foundation of all successful labor for Christ. But the power of this agency as used by any individual believer, is it not in exact proportion to his internal holiness? *This makes prayer prevalent.* "If ye *abide* in me, and my words *abide* in you, ye shall ask what ye will, and it shall be done unto you." "The effectual fervent prayer of a *righteous man* availeth much." *This makes prayer importunate.* It is only the heart deeply pervaded with the love of Christ that will "continue instant in prayer." With a vague and superficial desire for the salvation of men, Christians soon become weary of supplicating God in their behalf. *This prompts to the duty itself.* Minds full of God are constantly looking up to God. Holiness being from heaven, its possessor is ever seeking to revert to its source. In the very midst of earthly toil, mature Christians oftentimes seize, for their own indulgence, opportunities to pray, and are ever springing up to those eminences of meditation where they love to dwell.

"In the apostolic epistles, critics have observed that *doxologies* are sometimes imbedded in passages of remonstrance and of warning. It would seem that the sanctified minds of their authors came down unwillingly or from a sense of duty only, to deal with the sins and weaknesses of earth, and were continually on the watch for chances to rise like a bird let loose, though but for a moment, into the upper air."*

But second only to prayer, as an instrument for evangelism, is the indirect but powerful influence of example. Paul, in counselling his friend Timothy "as to the best method of doing good in the sphere of duty allotted to him," seems to give this the precedent even of teaching: "Take heed *unto thyself*,

---

* Still Hour, p. 98.

and unto the doctrine." "To be duly effective, truth must come not like incense from the censer that only holds it, but like fragrance from a flower, exhaling from a nature suffused with it throughout."

Neander, in his "Memorials of Christian Life," thus speaks of the influence of example in apostolic times: "By a continued succession of miracles Christianity could not have taken a firm hold on human nature, if it had not penetrated it by its divine power, and thus verified itself to be indeed that which alone can satisfy the higher necessities of the inner man. This divine power of the gospel revealed itself to the heathen in the lives of Christians, which 'showed forth the virtues of Him who had called them out of darkness into His marvellous light.' This announcement of the gospel by the *life* operated even more powerfully than its announcement by the *word*."

But how can this be, apart from the continual indwelling of God's Spirit? The *whole* power for good of example, can any thing be more evident than that it lies in inward sanctification? Indeed, without this, its influence so benign becomes one entirely of evil. "If therefore the light that is in thee be darkness, how great is that darkness!" A rocky coast on which government has erected a light-house, is for that very reason all the more dangerous if the lamp upon its summit be unlighted. An instrument of life, it is then changed into an instrument of death. Thus is it with a professed disciple of Christ who, unsanctified in heart, is ungodly in life. He lures men on to destruction, instead of guiding them in the way of salvation. He authenticates the way to death, and gives a sort of sacredness to the broad road. Those Christians only "shine as lights in the world," and, like the colossal statue at the harbor of Rhodes, "hold forth the word of life," who are "blameless and harmless, the sons of God without rebuke in the midst of a crooked and perverse nation."

And then, as to a *third* instrumentality that the Church may employ for evangelism, *oral and written instruction*, though we cannot deny that true and holy words may be spoken by lips untrue and profane, we are yet ready to assert that an experimental acquaintance with divine truth, or, in other words, inward piety, is the first qualification of every religious teacher, and the surest pledge of his success.

Dr. Caird, in one of his sermons, has expressed this thought so beautifully and forcibly that we need make no apology for the length of the quotation: "The conveyance of thought and feeling from mind to mind is not a process which depends on mere verbal accuracy. Language is not the only medium through which moral convictions and impressions are transmitted from speaker to hearer. There is another and more subtle mode of communication, a mysterious moral contagion, by means of which, irrespective of the mere intellectual apparatus employed, the instructor's beliefs and emotions are passed over into the minds of his auditory. Strong conviction has a force of persuasion irrespective of the mere oral instrument by which it works. Through the rudest forms of speech, originality and earnestness make themselves felt; and a sentence of simple, earnest *talk* will sometimes thrill the heart which the most refined and labored rhetoric would leave untouched. . . . No stereotyped orthodoxy, no stimulated fervors, however close and clever the imitation, will achieve the magic effects of reality. The preacher may reproduce *verbatim* the language of the wise and good, . . . but so long as they are but the echo of other men's experience, and not the expression of his own, the profoundest truths will fall ineffectively from his lips. There will be an unnaturalness and unreality in the very tone and manner in which he utters them. . . . The rod is not in the magician's hand, and it will not conjure. . . . The shape and semblance and color of truth he may display, but it will be as the waxen imitation of the lilies of the field; the divine aroma will not be there."

Dr. Chalmers was *intellectually* the same man when in Kilmany and in Glasgow, but *spiritually* very different. A mere moralist in the first place, with no personal and experimental acquaintance with Christ as his Saviour; a truly devout and spiritually-minded man in the last city, living in habitual communion with the infinite Truth and Life. And does not this go far to explain the fact that his ministry at Kilmany was barren and unfruitful; while at Glasgow, multitudes through his instrumentality were brought to Jesus?

And this suggests—as illustrating still

further the connection between *doing good* and *being good*—the simple mention of the fact, so much upon the very surface of the Church's history that no one can fail to notice it, that so many of her most useful members have been those whose birth was lowly, who spent their lives in poverty, and who were comparatively ignorant of this world's learning.

Howard, the great philanthropist, could not write English grammatically;* Robert Raikes, the founder of Sunday-schools, was a printer; John Pounds, the man who established the first ragged-school in London, was a cobbler; Leonhard Dober, the Moravian, who offered to sell himself into bondage that he might preach Christ to the enslaved upon the island of St. Thomas, and who has been called "the father of modern missions," was a potter; and there are few men, in any walk of life, who, having turned

---

* Bayne's Christian Life, p. 115.

many to righteousness, will like a star, in the firmament of God's redeemed people, shine as brightly as Harlan Page, the joiner.

But we have one more view of our theme to present. Of the precise and definite work assigned by our blessed Lord to the Christian ministry, we have this inspired statement: "And He gave some apostles, and some prophets, and some evangelists, and some pastors and teachers, for the perfecting of the saints, for the work of the ministry, for the edifying of the body of Christ." Here the whole work of a gospel minister is spoken of as something *within the Church and upon the saints*. Not one word is said of labor among the ungodly. His entire office, as here represented, is the perfection and edification of God's people. And is there no significance in this?

That we are not from it to infer that every minister should not labor directly and earnestly for the salvation of the impenitent, is indeed evident. For this is, after all, the ultimate purpose of all his toil. The passage instructs us only as to the best way of securing this end, and teaches us most impressively that this is through the upbuilding in holiness of God's people. Men are wont, we know, to feel that all the converting power of the Church is in the pulpit; but the sacred Scriptures tell us that it is in the body of Christ. It is not the ministry, but the Church, that is God's appointed instrumentality for the world's conversion.

And the experience of all ages confirms this truth. The ministry which fails to edify and perfect the people of God fails also in its attempts to convert sinners. Negligent and impotent in its work within the Church, it is likewise unsuccessful without it. Moreover, it is confessedly by the labors, prayers, and pious example of *private Christians* that a large majority of all the converts of all past ages have been brought to Christ.

HOLINESS AND USEFULNESS. 173

The relation of the ministry to the conversion of men is much more frequently *indirect* than *direct*. It stimulates to a closer walk with God, and to the cultivation of all the graces of Christianity, those believers whose personal influence and faithful endeavors bring men to Jesus, and *thus saves them;* oftener than by its most impassioned appeals to the impenitent it persuades them immediately to come to Christ.

The palm-tree—a Scriptural illustration, as in another connection we have remarked, of the believer's life—is an *evergreen*, and is continually bearing fruit. Though every thing around it may be parched with the summer's drought, and the very earth itself be as sterile as the desert, yet its leaves never wither, nor does it ever fail to afford both refreshment and shade to the weary traveller. And the reason lies in the single fact that, striking its roots deep down into the bowels of the earth, it draws its life from those springs of water that there never cease to flow.

What that tree is to an Oriental landscape, is the deeply devout believer to human society. Drawing his spiritual life from habitual communion with God, he is entirely unaffected by those spiritual droughts which destroy the usefulness of other Christians. He is an evergreen in the Church, and is continually bringing forth fruit to the glory of God.

CHAPTER XI.

PROGRESS IN RELIGION ESSENTIAL TO PREVENT DECLENSION.

> "Even as the soil which April's gentle showers
> Have filled with sweetness and enriched with flowers,
> Rears up her sucking plants, still shooting forth
> The tender blossoms of her timely birth,
> But if denied the beams of cheerly May.
> They hang their withered heads, and fade away;
> So man assisted by the Almighty's hand,
> His faith doth flourish and securely stand;
> But left a while, forsook, as in a shade,
> It languishes, and, nipped with sin, doth fade."—QUARLES.

"For if ye do these things, ye shall never *fall*."—2 PETER, 1: 10.

NOTHING saddens us so much in the history of good men as their frequent lapses into sin. We can hardly refrain from tears in reading of Noah's drunkenness, David's adultery, Jonah's petulance, and Peter's double crime of profanity and base denial of his Master. That men who have never "tasted and seen that the Lord is good" should not still desire communion with Him, is strange; but stranger still is the fact that *Christians* should ever forsake God and go again after idols. It is as if a savage who had been civilized should desire to return to his life in the wilderness, or as if the prodigal who had been restored to his father and home should try again to live on the husks that the swine eat.

But these instances of open and flagrant sin on the part of God's people are very few in comparison with their secret, though not less real, backslidings. Motives of worldly expediency are potent enough to keep men from letting their feet fall into the ways of sin, even if their hearts are there. We know of no great crimes of which the Galatians were guilty; yet so far in their affections had they departed from God as to account His servant Paul their enemy, and to constrain from him the inquiry, "Where is then the blessedness ye spake of?" And the same was true of the Christians at Ephesus. They had a commendable zeal against heresy and immorality—"hated the deeds of the Nicolaitans," and "could not bear them which were evil"—at the very time that they had "left their first love."

But whence these many and sad instances of religious declension? Is it enough to resolve them all into the one great fact of human frailty, and say that they are what we must ever expect to find in one so liable to fall as man?

Should we carefully examine any particular case of backsliding in the Church that might be presented us, we would find that its real cause was the want of a constant growth in all the graces of the believer's life. At some point the character was deficient, there had been no progress, and *there* the fall occurred.

Thus, Noah and David sinned, the one in

his intoxication and the other in his adultery, because they had not added to their faith *temperance,*—the subjection of all passion and appetite to the soul's highest good; Jonah and Elijah sinned in the complaints that they uttered against the ways of God towards them, and in their common prayer for death, because they had not added to their faith *patience,*—an implicit confidence in God; Peter sinned in his base denial of Christ, because he had not added to his faith *virtue,*—a true manly courage; and Paul and Barnabas sinned in that sharp contention about Mark which caused them to separate one from the other, because they had not added to their faith *brotherly kindness.* Indeed, what could on this point be more positive than that declaration of inspiration: "*If ye do these things,*"—if you diligently cultivate *all* the graces of Christianity,—"*ye shall never fall*"?

When a Christian who has failed to adorn

his character with every grace goes out into the battle of life, he is just like a mailed knight of olden times meeting his enemy with his visor down, or his helmet off, or his greaves loose, or his breastplate unfastened. He has in his character vulnerable points. Is it any wonder that he is pierced by the arrows of his great adversary? The promise of being "able to withstand in the evil day" is only made to those who take unto themselves "the whole armor of God."

It is often said of the Christian life, that men who are in it cannot remain stationary; that they are continually advancing in holiness and in preparation to meet God, or as continually going back to the world in their affections and interests. And the remark is as true as it is solemn and weighty. The question with a Christian is never, Shall I grow in grace, or remain with my present measure of sanctification? God has given no man such an election. Our choice is entirely between progression and retrogression, between going upward and going downward, between becoming spiritually-minded and becoming worldly-minded.

Is this not so? Take a small fraction of the believer's probation,—a single hour, if you please,—and see how impossible it is that we should live even for so short a time as this without our moral character experiencing some change. That hour brought with it solemn commands from God. Were they obeyed? The soul's spiritual strength was renewed. Were they disregarded? The consciousness of Jehovah's claim upon our obedience was weakened. That hour had its temptations. Though spent in the utmost privacy, away from the gaze of the world and its fascinations, yet in the presence of our own wicked desires and lusts, we heard their siren voice luring us on to evil. And did we manfully resist? What an element of strength was thus silently wrought into our character! what a true advance in holiness did we make! Or, on the contrary, were we overcome? How much was our power of resisting other temptations thus weakened! That hour brought some work for us to do. It laid a duty at our feet. Did we joyfully rise up and perform it, or, the hour expired, was the duty there still undone? The answer will decide what was the spiritual result upon us of that small portion of probation. If the duty was at once faithfully met, it gave robustness and vigor to our piety; but if wickedly neglected, we came out of that hour with our spiritual nature stunted and dwarfed.

An analogy that will illustrate this truth is found in the development of the intellect. It never stands still. Progression or retrogression is its universal law. No man is mentally to-day what he was yesterday, nor will he be to-morrow what he is to-day. The horizon of his knowledge widens or narrows, and his power of comprehending and communicating truth increases or lessens. A linguist will soon forget a language acquired after the most laborious study, if he never either speak or read it. Skill in the use of the pencil and chisel is rapidly lost when they are entirely laid aside. Scientific information disappears when scientific research is abandoned. In the world of letters, should a man imagine that he had made sufficient advancement, and for this reason resign himself to mental indolence, he would soon become a mere sciolist. The price of retaining what we know, is always to seek to know more. We preserve our learning and mental power only by increasing them.

And just as this becomes to a scholar a most impressive motive for constant study, ought the correlative fact in our spiritual life to constrain the Christian to a constant growth in grace. We cannot afford to allow a single day of life to pass without some advancement in religion, when we know that the inevitable consequence of failure is spiritual decline.

A man in a boat upon the rapids just above a cataract will not pause a moment in plying diligently his oars. For he well knows that there is no such thing as standing still in that river. Every moment of rest in his rowing only allows his boat to glide for a little way down the stream, putting in jeopardy his life or increasing his toil in the future. Our souls in a situation not unlike to this, in a position where not to advance is necessarily to go back, how strange that Christians should ever remit their exertions! that they should not be "steadfast, unmovable, *always abounding in the* work of the Lord"!

CHAPTER XII.

ASSURANCE OF HOPE—ITS RELATIONS TO SANCTIFICATION.

> " 'Tis a point I long to know;
> Oft it causes anxious thought.
> Do I love the Lord, or no?
> Am I His, or am I not?
>
> *   *   *   *   *
>
> Lord, decide the doubtful case;
> Thou who art thy people's Sun,
> Shine upon thy work of grace,
> If it be indeed begun."
>
>   NEWTON.

"And we desire that every one of you do show the same diligence to the *full assurance of hope* unto the end."—HEB. 6: 11.

THE land of Canaan promised by God to the posterity of Abraham, it is not strange that the patriarch, in his earnest desire for some confirmation of his faith, should have asked, "Lord God, whereby shall I know that I shall inherit it?" The goodliness of the land, the fact that he was then childless, and that a strong nation possessed it, all conspired to prompt the inquiry and to make it both natural and proper. The miracle, also, that God wrought in reply, clearly evinced the reasonableness of the request.

But if Abraham, with the promise of the earthly Canaan, longed to know *assuredly* that it would be his, a similar desire is felt by every aspirant after its great antitype, *heaven*. We do but express in words what every Christian in his heart feels, when in their behalf we repeat the inquiry, "Whereby shall I know that I shall inherit it?" Nor, although the days of visions and dreams are over, need we despair of having this question satisfactorily answered.

We all know that a "full assurance of hope" has in this life been attained by some saints. Inspired biography is full of such instances. They lie all along the line of the Church's history, from the time of Job, who in the confidence of his faith exclaimed, "*I* know that *my* Redeemer liveth, and that He shall stand at the latter day upon the earth," to Paul, who with equal boldness could say, "For to me to live is Christ, and to die is gain." And surely whatever heights of piety any of God's people may in a past age have attained, it is the privilege of Christians now to reach.

Moreover, were it impossible for men ever to arrive at a certain knowledge of their personal acceptance with God, why in His word is it so frequently commanded? Of what utility would obedience to such an injunction as this be, "Examine yourselves, whether ye be in the faith; prove your own selves," if, after all the introspection, we could arrive at no definite conclusion with reference to our true spiritual condition?

In applying, then, the inquiry of Abraham with regard to the earthly Canaan to the hope of heaven that as Christians we cherish, we repeat the remark that it is no impracticable question that we propose. It is the privilege of every believer to attain even in this life a full assurance of his personal acceptance by Christ and his heirship in the inheritance of the saints. "Being justified by faith, we have peace with God, through our Lord Jesus Christ; by whom also we have access by faith into this grace wherein we stand, and *rejoice* in hope of the glory of God." Conscious of great weakness and sin, and knowing not what shall betide him in the future, the Christian may yet, looking down the line of his life, and seeing its end on that bed of trembling where his breath grows shorter, and his blood stops, and the whole tabernacle of his flesh begins to crumble, exclaim, "I know in whom I have believed, and am persuaded that He is able to keep that which I have committed unto Him against that day."

And how blessed is such a condition!

An inhabitant of earth, but a *certain* heir of heaven; a poor mortal, but "the Spirit itself bearing witness with his spirit that he is a child of God." Can a higher felicity than this be imagined? An old writer, speaking of faith as the ring that the bridegroom of the Church places upon the finger of all chosen to be His bride, says of a full assurance of hope, "that it may be considered as the brilliant, or the cluster of brilliants, which adorn the ring, and make it incomparably more beautiful and valuable." And this diamond of full assurance in the golden ring of faith, "the believer's felicity," he adds, "is only inferior to that of just spirits made perfect in heaven."

But the certain knowledge of our acceptance by Christ within the reach of every believer, how is it to be attained? By the memory of *by-gone experience?* By the ability of recalling a moment in the past of *marked conversion?* How almost universal is this mode of deciding the question, "Am I a Christian?" A certificate of election into Christ's kingdom, it is supposed, must read thus: "One, two, three, or more years ago, I was the subject of a great change. Christ met me in the way of sin, as He met Saul on the road to Damascus, and, though I heard no voice, and saw no light that blinded me, as he did, yet I had then new and very peculiar feelings; and was not that the new birth? Did not Christ then commence a work of grace upon my heart? and, as grace always completes what it begins, may I not confidently conclude that I am a child of God?" Of *present* experience, of what is *now* the soul's *actual condition*, not one word is said: all *is an experience exhumed* from the past.

How hazardous with such a certificate to come up to the pearly gates of the New Jerusalem and to hope therein to gain admission! We would not, indeed, have men entirely forget the day when they supposed themselves to have entered upon the divine life,—if of that time they have *any distinct remembrance*,—nor would we have them altogether exclude their experience at that time from their decision of the question of their present interest in Christ. It doubtless forms a *single fact* that should then be considered; but hardly more. Upon it the great question of our acceptance with God can never turn. Christianity cannot be in the soul as a matter of history only, but always of present and living experience.

And equally dangerous with this is the attempt to decide the question of our personal call and election into Christ's kingdom by the occasional enjoyment of *rapturous religious emotion*. No one, in reading the biographies of good men, can have failed to notice the fact that God sometimes, in the fulness of His kindness, seems in a very special and peculiar way to manifest Himself to

His people. He comes very near to them. He soothes their heart. He encourages them. He feeds them with the grapes of Eshcol, and almost gives them a vision of their eternal home. Perhaps they are alone, in the struggle of a closet-prayer; and as their earnest cry ascends to God, the voice comes back, "Be of good cheer: thy sins are forgiven thee." Perhaps they are in some difficult service, where temptations beat so hard upon them that they are afraid, and, as they stand trembling and ready to sink, God says to them, "Fear not, thou worm Jacob: I am with thee." Perhaps they are sick, nigh unto death, and, while God shakes their bones over the sepulchre, He teaches them to exclaim, "I know that if my earthly house of this tabernacle is dissolved, I have a building of God, an house not made with hands, eternal in the heavens." How beautifully does Coleridge describe such seasons in the Christian's life!

> "In some hour of solemn jubilee,
> The massy gates of Paradise are thrown
> Wide open, and forth come, in fragments wild,
> Sweet echoes of unearthly melodies,
> And odors snatched from beds of amaranth,
> And they that from the crystal river of life
> Sprung up on freshened wing, ambrosial gales!
> The favored good man in his lonely walk
> Perceives them, and his silent spirit drinks
> Strange bliss, which he shall recognize in heaven."

But to the enjoyment of seasons like these shall a man look for the *conclusive evidence* of his being in a gracious state? Are we for the full assurance of hope to depend upon the memory of such prelibations of heavenly bliss? Observe how much here depends upon constitutional temperament, and how much more likely men of keen sensibility and lively imagination are to have such experiences than those of a cold and phlegmatic disposition!

Moreover, in the realm of mere emotion, we are here just where we may be most easily self-deceived. There are other influences besides the Divine Spirit, capable of operating most powerfully upon the feelings. An impassioned description of heaven, united with pathetic appeals and fervent exhortations, has sometimes filled an ungodly mind not only with an earnest desire for its happiness, but with a rapturous joy that seemed to it almost like a foretaste of glory.

But if "assurance of hope" is in neither of these ways to be attained, where is it to be found? What will *warrant the confident conviction* that we are the friends of God, and *certify our election* into the kingdom of His Son? *We answer emphatically, our sanctification, the soul's increase in inward holiness, its possession of all the graces of the new life.* In a man's certificate of Christian character is there not one word said of his experience at conversion, nor yet any mention made of his subsequent rapturous emotions, but do we simply read, "Faith, Virtue, Knowledge, Temperance, Patience, Godliness, Brotherly Kindness, Charity, these things are in him and abound," how can any doubt his acceptance with Christ? The possession of these graces "MAKES HIS CALLING AND ELECTION SURE."

Some days before Columbus caught a glimpse of the New World, land-birds of beautiful plumage hovered round his ships and filled the air with their sweet music. Certain harbingers of his great discovery! How did the courage of his disheartened crew revive at the sight! They knew now that their perilous voyage would not be in vain, that the long-looked-for land was just before them, and that they had won for themselves an immortality of glory. An office not unlike this is performed by the graces of Christianity to the voyager who on the ocean of life is sailing to eternity. Beholding his character adorned with these graces,—seeing these birds of Paradise careering on bright wings around him,—he cannot doubt that he is bound heavenward, that he is nearing his home, and that he will finally enter upon its everlasting felicity.

"Full assurance of hope" is, then, to be obtained only by a persevering effort to lead a holy life. It is a flower that we pluck as we struggle on in the rugged pathway of our sanctification. It is when we become more and more Christ-like, get new victories over sin, bridle lust and evil passion more perfectly, in a word, come nearer and nearer to God, that He comes nearer to us, and, embracing us in His paternal arm, enables us across the Jordan to behold the celestial Canaan as *our* home.

CHAPTER XIII.

HOLINESS HERE—ITS CONNECTION WITH GLORY HEREAFTER.

> "Who are these in bright array,
>   This innumerable throng,
> Round the altar night and day
>   Hymning one triumphant song?
> *   *   *   *   *   *
> These through fiery trials trod;
>   These from great affliction came:
> Now, before the throne of God,
>   Sealed with His almighty name,
> Clad in raiment pure and white,
>   Victor palms in every hand,
> Through their dear Redeemer's might,
>   More than conquerors they stand."
> MONTGOMERY.

"And behold I come quickly; and my reward is with me, to give every man *according as his work shall be.*"—REV. 22: 12.

THE sacred Scriptures reveal nothing for the mere gratification of curiosity. Every thing that is *practically* necessary to be known, with a view to its influence on the heart and conduct, they teach with the utmost simplicity and directness; but further than that they seldom go. "A lighthouse on a dark and stormy coast," they show us where the port is, and how we must steer our vessel if we would hope to enter it in safety; but of the cities or green fields which spread themselves around it, and of the people who inhabit them, they reveal to us almost nothing.

And, bitter as may be the disappointment that this reticence occasions, it still, clearly, furnishes us with no valid objection to the Bible's inspiration. Indeed, it is an evidence of its divine origin. An impostor or a mere enthusiast would have been exceeding garrulous upon such a theme as heaven. He would have *enlarged* on all the particulars of a future life, and would have given us the most lively and glowing description of things so interesting to curiosity. And who can say that to afford us this evidence of the divinity of God's word is not one of the reasons for "the *brief, dry,* and *general* language of Scripture on these points"?

But let us not speak of the revelations of the Bible with reference to the believer's future home as if they were *wholly* confined to the simple point of how it may be reached. Our *personal and practical interest* in heaven wider than this, so are the teachings of inspiration.

To afford both encouragement to the zealous Christian and alarm to the negligent, two facts—with others—are plainly taught us in the sacred Scriptures with reference to the eternal abode of the righteous.

1. There is not among the saved in heaven a *perfect equality of glory and happiness.* All saints *full* both of honor and blessedness, all have not the same capacity for either. "And they that be wise" (teachers) "shall shine as the brightness of the firmament; and they that turn many to righteous-

ness, as the stars for ever and ever." "There is one glory of the sun, and another glory of the moon, and another glory of the stars; for one star differeth from another star in glory. So also is the resurrection of the dead."

2. This diversity of glory and happiness among saints hereafter will be both occasioned and measured by the difference in their holiness and usefulness in this life. "He which soweth *sparingly* shall reap also *sparingly;* and he which soweth *bountifully* shall reap also *bountifully.*" "Behold, I come quickly, and my reward is with me, to give every man *according as his work shall be.*" "If we *suffer*, we shall also *reign* with Him." In Christ's parable of the pounds—which was evidently intended to convey to us some knowledge respecting our final judgment—we find that the reward bestowed by the nobleman upon his servants, *intrusted with the same deposit,*

was in every case exactly measured by the improvement that they made of it. The man who turned his trust to a *tenfold* improvement, and he who gained with his pound *five* others, were rewarded, successively, by a *ten* and a *five fold* authority.

And these facts with reference to heaven, as they are revealed for our encouragement and warning, so are they to this end frequently employed by the sacred penmen. Christian teachers, *in this day,* seem to be afraid to speak of the rewards of heaven as *proportioned* by the good works that believers here perform. They hesitate to employ this motive as a stimulus to Christian activity, lest in some minds they might thus weaken belief in that great cardinal truth of *justification by faith alone.* But the apostles and early preachers of Christianity had no such fear. They were covetous of a *high place* in heaven for all among whom they labored; and, knowing that this was the *reward* of faithfulness here, they were constantly stimulating their hearers by such a prize to a life both of holiness and usefulness. By this motive they pointed even their exhortations to pecuniary liberality,—the very lowest and easiest form of beneficence: "Charge them that are rich in this world . . . that they do good, that they be rich in good works, ready to distribute, willing to communicate: laying up in store for themselves a *good foundation* against the time to come, that they may lay hold on *eternal life.*"

A radical distinction, however, should in this connection be observed between the prize held out to the Christian, and all the glory and greatness of this world. "In the present life, the highest objects of ambition, and those which men most eagerly strive after, are such as, *by their nature*, can only be attained by a few. That there should be any who are wealthy, powerful, and celebrated, implies a necessity that there should be others who are poor, subjects, and obscure. That all, or even the greater part, of any community should be rich men, or rulers, or eminent, is not only impossible, but inconceivable."

But this is not so of that prize which should excite the ambition of God's people. A *few* cannot win it to the exclusion of the rest. The *elevation* of one saint in heaven does not imply the *depression* of another. The power and splendor and riches of that better world may be enjoyed by an unlimited number, and by each in proportion to his fitness for it. In the race for most worldly objects, "they which run, run *all;* but *one* receiveth the prize:" in the pursuit of heavenly blessings, *all* may so run as to obtain.

Here, then, is the motive with which we would now urge Christian believers to a "*closer walk*" with God. No real progress in religion, no increase of personal holiness, ever made in this world, will be unnoticed or unrewarded by God. Growing in grace here, and ever ascending in moral character nearer and nearer to God, we are thus continually adding new jewels to the crown of our everlasting rejoicing, and preparing for ourselves a high place of glory and blessedness in heaven.

> " If in some fair and jewelled crown
>   That to the blest redeemed is given,
> Are stars that cast their brightness down,
>   *Loveliest* among the gems of heaven,
> It is the diadem he wears"

whose whole character on earth has been the most perfectly transformed into the image of Christ.

And this motive to sanctification we have reserved as the triumphant climax of our argument, because it is thus reserved in the sacred Scriptures. At the close of the brief but comprehensive summary of the motives by which Peter enforces his exhortation to diligence in the cultivation of all the graces of Christianity, we read, "*For so* an entrance shall be ministered unto you *abundantly* into the everlasting kingdom of our Lord and Saviour Jesus Christ."

We have already had occasion to refer to the figure that in the Greek underlies the word which is here translated "*ministered*," and for which in the fifth verse of the same chapter we read "*add*." The reference is to those choirs of trained artists which the opulent private citizens of Athens gratuitously furnished to the magnificent shows of the state. When into that splendid capital of Greece, and to its senate-house, some distinguished warrior or statesman made his triumphant entrance, a whole band of musicians welcomed him. He was escorted into the city with every possible mark of respect. He had an "*abundant entrance ministered unto him.*"

And thus, says the apostle, shall it be with the Christian who has here been diligent to add to his faith all the other graces of the divine life. He will have a "triumphant outgate from earth, and a magnificent entrance into paradise." It will be with him as if a radiant train of holy minstrels should escort him to the mansions of immortal glory and blessedness. The gates of heaven will be thrown wide open at his approach, and joyfully will he be admitted to the felicity of the New Jerusalem.

Bunyan, ever true to the teachings of inspiration, gives us in his inimitable allegory a striking illustration both of this truth and its counterpart. "Christian," in his pilgrimage, was guilty of many relapses into sin. He listened to the counsel of Mr. Worldly-Wiseman, and turned to go for help to Mount Sinai. He fell asleep in the arbor and lost his roll out of his bosom; and, though warned by the shepherds upon the Delectable Mountains of "*the Flatterer*," yet to his temptation did he yield. And so in "*the river*" Christian had "great distresses." He could hardly keep his "head above water." He sometimes lost "all sight of the city that was beyond," and had a long struggle before he found in the river "ground to stand upon."

How different from this is the narrative of Mr. *Stand-fast*, a man whose name indicates his character, and who is represented by Bunyan as having always abounded in the work of the Lord! What an abundant entrance into heaven was ministered to him! Let me quote a few sentences from the Dreamer's account of his death: "And now the time being come for him to haste away, there was a *great calm* in the river; wherefore Mr. Stand-fast, when he was about half-way in, stood a while and talked with his companions that had waited upon him thither. And he said, This river hath been a terror to many: yea, the thoughts of it also have often frightened me; but now methinks I stand easy. . . . The waters, indeed, are to the palate bitter, and to the stomach cold; yet the thoughts of what I am going to, and of the convoy that waits for me on the other side, do lie as a glowing coal at my heart. I see myself now at the end of my journey; my toilsome days are ended. I am going to see the head which was crowned with thorns, and that face which was spit upon for me. I have formerly lived by hearsay and faith: but now I go where I shall live by sight, and shall be with Him in whose company I delight myself. I have loved to hear my Lord spoken of; and wherever I have seen the print of His shoe in the earth, there I have coveted to set my foot too. His name has been to me as a civet-box, yea, sweeter than all perfumes. . . . Now while he was thus in discourse, his countenance changed, his strong man bowed under him, and after that he had said, Take me, for I come unto Thee, he ceased to be seen of them."

"At the convent of Mount Sinai, the monks, ever watchful against their enemies, admit guests one by one, hoisting them by a basket into a lofty window through the wall; but when a visitor arrives with a special letter from the head of their order at Cairo, the huge gates of the convent are unbarred, and the cavalcade ride through the ample portal and up the paved court, where the monks are drawn up in order to welcome the guest, who is conducted to the principal chamber and attended with every mark of respect."* Something not unlike this we may suppose to occur in the entrance of believers into their final home in heaven. Some "are saved as by fire." They "scarcely" get into the kingdom. They

---

* The Christian Graces, p. 276.

enter heaven as by the "postern gate." While at the approach of others we may well imagine the angels as exclaiming, "Lift up your heads, O ye gates, and be ye lifted up, ye everlasting doors," and receive this trophy of the Saviour's love.

CHAPTER XIV.

HOLINESS THE GREAT NECESSITY OF THE CHURCH.

"No careful reader of the New Testament, and observer of the present state of the Church, can fail to be convinced that what she now wants is a high spirituality. The Christian profession is sinking in its tone of piety; the line of separation between the Church and the world becomes less and less perceptible; and the character of genuine Christianity, as expounded from pulpits and delineated in books, has too rare a counterpart in the lives and spirit of its professors."—REV. J. A. JAMES.

"The Church itself requires conversion."—HARRIS.

"Christendom itself must be more thoroughly Christianized before Heathendom will relinquish its old character and worship."—WILLIAMS.

SHOULD we remark that the Church of Christ is now accomplishing but feebly and imperfectly the great ends of her organization, we would only utter a sentiment to the truthfulness of which every pious heart would instantly respond. Like a ponderous engine, the Church is now creeping silently over rails that she ought to shake by the might of her irresistible movement; or, like an immense factory, perfect in all the details of its machinery, she is achieving but little compared with the scope and finish of her structure. Zion is not in our day as aggressive upon an ungodly world as she once was, or as from her predicted successes we might reasonably expect. Converts to the truth do not now "fly as clouds, and doves to their windows." Great social and political evils do not disappear before the triumphal march of Christianity, nor is heathendom being *rapidly* subjugated to the sway of the Redeemer.

That the Church has accomplished, even within the memory of some now living, great and glorious things, and that in view of them we ought to take courage and rejoice, we cheerfully concede. Going back to the time when Bishop Butler said that he "did not know of a learned man in England who believed in the plenary inspiration of the sacred Scriptures," or to that when even a professed minister of Christ poured contempt upon missions to the heathen and stigmatized one of the first heralds of salvation to India as a "consecrated cobbler"; and contrasting with that the present condition of Christianity both in the schools of science and on heathen shores, we are constrained to exclaim, *What hath God wrought!* But these victories, what are they, to the triumphs which still remain to be won? Is not Satan still the God of this world? Is not the broad way still the thronged way? Christendom compared, either geographically, or with reference to the number of her population, with heathendom, is she not small and almost insignificant? Do not our hearts sink within us when the simple statistics upon this subject are presented us?

Nor, when from this view of the *comparative inefficiency* of the Church—a view the correctness of which no one can doubt—we come to inquire as to the cause, can we long hesitate in our reply.

Wide-spread *doctrinal errors* have, in days past, shorn the Church of much of her strength. But certainly it is not so now. Confessing that there may exist in our religious teaching a lack of vigor of statement and clearness of elucidation, there is yet, it must be conceded, no radical unsoundness in it, working its destructive influences at the very core of piety. Our creeds are Scriptural; and when men abandon them, they usually receive as their reward little else than the virtuous indignation of the good.

Religious disputations once consumed no small portion of the Church's energy. Men discussed questions of predestination and election, free will and sovereignty, with an acrimony that led to personal and life-long alienations and that brought great dishonor upon religion. Divines were then "famous according as they had lifted up axes upon the thick trees." But now theological controversies are, to a great extent, at an end. The disciples of Calvin and Arminius, Cranmer and Knox, in our day live side by side in peace.

Heretofore the energies of the Church have been somewhat impeded by the want of proper organizations. Christians who desired to do any thing for their Master were constrained to act *alone*, or, at best, in very small companies. There were then no arrangements for consolidating the activities of the Church, and bringing them all together to bear upon any single point. But now so complete and comprehensive are our plans of Christian exertion that no effort in any department of labor need ever be made alone or in vain. The net-work of the Church's charities cover the whole field of man's moral destitution; and *her life* is connected by so many wires with the whole life of humanity, that any of her myriad members may, if they please, be put into a communication of beneficence with their entire race.

Nor, still again, is it possible to charge the present inefficiency of the Church upon any want in the number, wealth, intelligence, and social standing of her members. Estimated by any law of mere worldly measurement, the Church, as an institution designed to influence society, cannot be despised. Zion numbers among her professed members *millions* of our race. She has an average proportion of the world's wealth, and a very large share of its intelligence and commercial enterprise.

Where, then, is the point of her failure? What is the element of influence she wants? **Her** progress in the subjugation of this world to Christ, why is it so slow as oftentimes to sadden its anxious expectants, and so to embolden the enemies of the truth as to lead them to exclaim, "Where is now thy God?"

Our answer contains a serious charge against the Church of Christ, and one which ought not to be made without unmistakable evidence of its truth. There is in this day, among the professed people of God, a great want of *deep, thorough piety*. Christians are zealous, but not spiritually-minded; liberal, but not given to self-mortification; anxious to promote the extension of religion in the world, but strangely indifferent to its progress in their own souls. They linger too much around the mere rudiments of Christianity, and do not go on to perfection. They are satisfied with living at a great distance from God, and are too tolerant of personal imperfections. *Is it not so?*

In the Bible the Christian life is uniformly

spoken of as one of *self-denial and suffering*. The followers of Christ, according to His own declaration, "are to deny themselves, and *daily* to take up their cross." Jesus is an example to His people in His sufferings. Among the truthful and significant devices of the ancient Church employed to illustrate the position of believers in this world, was one representing a bullock standing between a plough and an altar, with the inscription, "*Ready for either.*" Would the facts of Christian experience in the modern Church allow the use of such a device? When men now unite with the people of God, do they feel that they must hold themselves in constant readiness either "to drag and swelter in the field of service, or to bleed on the altar of sacrifice"?

Self-denial is not with us the universal *law* of Christianity, but the occasional exception. The contributions of time and money that are made to the cause of Christ seldom reach the point of absolute *sacrifice*. It is the *leisure* that secular business *may* afford, or the *surplus* of an income that cannot well be expended on worldly luxuries, that is usually contributed to the extension of Christ's kingdom. "I give as much of my time and means to the Church as I *conveniently* can," is the almost boastful expression of many modern professors. Should God receive nothing for Himself save that which *costs the donor something,* how few of the gifts that His people now present to Him would be accepted!

Again, in the sacred Scriptures, Christians are represented as " a *peculiar people,*" and "*conformity to the world*" is most solemnly forbidden. But is this line of separation always perceptible? Do Christians never follow "the apish fashions of the world"? After a long acquaintance, have we never been almost startled by hearing that our friend was a member of some

Christian Church? Are "grand equipages," and "splendid entertainments," and all the pomp and vanity of "*high life,*" consistent with "*the simplicity that is in Christ*"?

We would remember that woe pronounced by our blessed Lord upon those who "offend one of His little ones." And we would not dare to exaggerate, even in the slightest degree, the faults of the Church, which is, after all, Christ's body. But are we not now uttering true and honest words, and words that we should write with tears, as Paul did his mournful message of the existence in the Church at Philippi of enemies to the cross of Christ? An occasional presence at the *communion-table,* is not that every thing which is "*peculiar*" and "*unworldly*" with multitudes of the professed followers of Christ?

But do our readers desire still further evidence of the sad fact that it is to the want of a deep, thorough piety in the

Church that we are to attribute her present comparative inefficiency, let them observe how all her wants *root themselves in this one,* and would be removed the very moment that this grand *defect was remedied.*

The Church needs an *increase of ministers.* "The harvest is plenteous, but the laborers are few." "Any religious body," however, as Isaac Taylor says, "within which there is *vitality,* will supply itself with an adequate proportion of ministers." In such an internal condition, it will need no external pressure to induce its sons to devote themselves to the work of preaching Christ. The ministry is the natural outgrowth of the life of the Church, and it cannot wane save as that life declines. Even should the sacred office be hedged about on every side with trials, and its occupants be in great peril of terminating their days by martyrdom, yet with a vigorous and healthy life in the Church many a mother would take her infant son, as did Nonna, the mother of Gregory Nazianzen, and joyfully dedicate him to this work; and many a young man, averting his gaze from all the tempting employments of secular life, would rejoice in the privilege of becoming a herald of the cross.

The Church is greatly in need of a larger and more liberal charity to all her benevolent institutions. "Lying now like Lazarus at the gate of Opulence, where Christians fare sumptuously every day, or like mendicants wandering among the churches and receiving only the shreds and parings of liberal incomes," these institutions need to be received at the *table* of God's people, and to be sustained and enlarged by their self-denying contributions. The clenched hand of avarice needs to be opened; and, instead of that poor pittance that men now dole out in charity to the Church, every man is to learn to give "*as the Lord hath prospered him."* Indeed, the whole *theory* of Christian stewardship needs to be put *into practice.* Men are to live out in their lives that truth "considered by all as so true that it has lost all the power of truth and lies bedridden in the dormitory of the soul."

But what can ever accomplish this but a deep and thorough work of grace upon the heart? What influence short of the continual indwelling of the Holy Spirit can uproot covetousness? Of the Macedonian Christians Paul says, "They gave their very selves to the Lord first." No wonder, then, that the riches of their liberality abounded in deep poverty. Their personal dedication to God solves the riddle of their noble charity.

The Church in our day pre-eminently needs powerful and wide-spread *revivals of religion.* Such seasons have been promised her. Pentecost was the earnest of their coming. Such seasons are seemingly absolutely essential to her final success. At the present rate of the Church's progress, the world would never be converted to Christ. We must wait the fulfilment of the promise that "a nation shall be born at once," before we can hope that Christ's kingdom will speedily come.

But of the advent of that day can we cherish any well-grounded expectation until we see a deepening piety and a sturdier vigor of principle among God's own people? Though Jehovah is a Sovereign, can we hope that He will ever abundantly pour out His Spirit upon the ungodly world while His Church is cold and worldly?

Here, then, we repeat it, is the great necessity of the Church in this day, *a deeper work* of grace in the hearts of her individual members. "A sickly and bedwarfed Christianity" will not furnish the requisite laborers or the needful funds for the world's conversion; nor with such a type of piety dare we hope for great outpourings of the

Spirit. What now we most need in the Church is *holy men*, men just as absorbed in winning souls to Christ as worldlings are in gathering gold; men who, in the touchingly beautiful language of one of the old Covenanters, "will all day long find nothing but Christ to rest in, and whose very sleep is a pursuing after Him in dreams, and who intensely desire to awake in His likeness." We need, as Christians, to make that motto adopted by that corp of young Romish priests, the Redemptorists, who are seeking to revive the rapidly waning power of the Papacy, our own: "All for thee, O Lord; O my Jesus, all for thee!" In this age which has written "*progress*" on its banners, and whose very watchword is "Onward," it will not do for Christianity to be the only thing that is not advancing.

Listen, then, fellow-disciples of Christ, to the powerful array of motives by which God would persuade you to a *closer walk* with

Him. It is your *duty.* "This is the will of God, even your sanctification." Your highest *usefulness* demands it. *You must be good to do good.* The perils of religious *declension* threaten you if you do not advance. If with you in the divine life there is no *progression,* there must be *retrogression.* The way of sanctification is the only way that leads to a "*full assurance of hope.*" To make your "calling and election sure," you must diligently cultivate in your life every grace of the Spirit. And each new step that you take in holiness here will add new lustre to that unfading crown of glory that awaits you in heaven.

Can you, then, hesitate? The potency of these motives, can you resist it? Heretofore indifferent to your progress in piety, can you now close this little volume and live as before? Have you still no longings of heart for a "closer walk" with God? We can only, in parting, leave these solemn questions with you.

"Now the God of peace, that brought again from the dead our Lord Jesus, that great Shepherd of the sheep, through the blood of the everlasting covenant, make you *perfect* in every good work to do His will, working in you that which is well pleasing in His sight, through Jesus Christ; to whom be glory for ever and ever. Amen."

THE END.

www.ingramcontent.com/pod-product-compliance
Lightning Source LLC
Chambersburg PA
CBHW021837230426
43669CB00008B/994